SOURDOUGH RECIPES COOKBOOK

A Step-By-Step Mastery Guide To No-Fail Baking And Crafting Healthful Breads, Sweets, And More With 120+ Recipes For All Skill Levels

GENEVIEVE WILKER

Copyright © 2024 by Genevieve Wilker

Disclaimer Notice

Thank You For Reading!

I hope you will enjoy reading it as much as I enjoyed writing it.

Your support means so much to me!

If you find value in these pages, I kindly ask you to consider supporting me with your feedback.

Your feedback not only helps me improve but also helps other readers discover this book.

YOUR GIFTS ARE WAITING FOR YOU!

To enhance your experience and to give you additional help, I have prepared some great bonuses for you!

Find download instructions at the end of the book.

I'm confident you'll love these additional resources!

Table of Contents

Introduction

Lots of us recall the house smelling like fresh bread. Many fear baking bread, especially sourdough. The mysterious "starter," timing, and expertise may intimidate. You may have tried before but got a hard, inedible brick. What if everyone could create delicious sourdough bread? I'm "Sourdough Recipes Cookbook: A Step-by-Step Mastery Guide to No-Fail Baking and Crafting Healthful Breads, Sweets, and More with 120+ Recipes for All Skill Levels."

Sourdough baking is simplified in this book. We know your typical issues and frustrations. The vocabulary and proportions of sourdough baking might be overwhelming. This book aims to change that. No matter your baking experience, this book will help you succeed and enjoy sourdough. Bakers of all skill levels can succeed and enjoy baking with our 120+ recipes.

Start by learning about ingredients and tools. We'll help you grow a sourdough starter, a live colony of wild yeast and bacteria needed for sourdough bread. Next, mix, shape, proof, and bake dough. Each chapter improves your skills, preparing you for complex recipes. Learn to detect properly proofed dough, discern over-kneaded from under-kneaded dough, and understand how temperature and humidity affect bread.

Why lead you this way? Sourdough baking took years to master. Flat loaves, temperamental sourdough starts, and complex recipes have plagued me, too. I learned sourdough baking via patience, study, and practice. This book contains my baking wisdom at all levels. Prepare for a memorable baking experience with your apron and mixing bowl. Sourdough mastery begins here.

Chapter 1: What is Sourdough?

Sourdough bread is popular because it's tasty, preserved well, and is healthy.

Sourdough appeared thousands of years ago and was crucial to bread-making until the Middle Ages. Beer barm and yeasts supplanted it.

Water, cereal flour, yeasts, and lactic acid bacteria make sourdough. Sometimes it labels religious bread.

Small levels of bread-making yeasts and bacteria cover wheat. By grinding grains into flour and adding water, these bacteria multiply. Maintain the correct temperature and make a "starter" with flour.

For bread to rise, yeast cells must emit CO_2. The bread's flavor, texture, and fragrance might benefit from yeast and enzymes.

The starter and bread are sourdough. Many choices exist between hard rye flour and water starts and milk and cornmeal air batters.

Lactobacilli and wild yeast work together in flour and adjacent areas after watering. These little creatures' flour-and-water slurry (starter) byproducts give bread a rich taste and rise.

Normal yeast and flour-borne bacteria form sourdough. Classic recipes require sourdough starter (water and wheat), salt, and powder. No leaven, butter, oils, or sugar. Delicious bread.

Anyone who has eaten sourdough will say its tang is unique. Sourdough bread has the same bacteria that make yogurt and sour cream pucker. Water activates it in wheat flour and yeast. The process is straightforward:

Natural enzymes in wheat flour and water make glucose. Tang bacteria + glucose = natural yeast food + leaven. Leaven + flour + water equals natural leaven.

Nature produces enough leaven (yeast) to raise bread. Pretty cool, huh? How could small produce such a great performance?

Sourdough is an ancient grain fermentation.

It was the main bread leavening until baker's yeast replaced it centuries ago. It originated in Egypt around 1,500 BC.

Grain fermentation produces gas, raising leavened bread.

Most leavened bread rises with commercial yeast. In traditional sourdough fermentation, "wild yeast" and lactic acid bacteria from wheat leaven bread.

Wild yeast avoids acidity better than bakers. That aids dough-making with lactic acid-producing bacteria.

Yogurt, kefir, pickles, sauerkraut, and kimchi contain lactic acid bacteria.

A sourdough "starter." contains wild yeast, lactic acid bacteria, flour, and water. Bread rises and tastes unique because the starter ferments sugars in the dough.

Sourdough bread ferments and expands, giving it a peculiar texture.

Sourdough bread is popular in Mediterranean, Middle Eastern, and San Francisco Bay countries.

Sourdough bread from the store may not be baked properly, limiting its health benefits.

Buy "real" sourdough from a farmer's market or artisan baker.

Sourdough is an ancient leavening bread. Wild yeast and flour-derived lactic acid bacteria leaven dough Instead of baker's yeast.

Chapter 2: Sourdough Storage

Use sourdough starter with this in mind.

How to store sourdough starter. Feeding your beginning once or twice a day works well.

Sourdough starters can be stored in plastic, glass, pint, or covered pots. Starting in the fridge is advised but not needed. You can even keep it in a dark, cool kitchen and only feed it.

If not immediately used, dry your beginning. Spread it thinly on two pieces of parchment paper with a spatula, let it dry at room temperature for a day or two, then peel it off and store it in a plastic bag until needed.

Keeping sourdough longer is easy. Use these tips to use sourdough effectively.

Starting with sourdough, preserving it, and using tips and tricks to make this gourmet experience easier, start baking.

Chapter 3: 120 Amazing Whole sourdough Recipes

1. 100% Whole Wheat Peanut Butter And Jelly Bread

- Serving: 12
- Prep: 10m
- Ready in: 2h50m

Ingredients

- 10 oz. water
- half a cup of peanut butter
- One-quarter cup light brown sugar
- Half a spoonful of strawberry jam
- Half a teaspoon of salt
- One-third tsp baking soda
- One-third tsp raising agent
- Vital Wheat Gluten, 3 tablespoons
- Three-thirds cup whole wheat flour
- half a tsp dry active yeast

Direction

1. Pour water, peanut butter, jelly, brown sugar, salt, baking soda, raising agent, gluten, 3 1/3 cups plus 1 tablespoon whole wheat flour, and yeast into the bread machine pan.
2. Add these ingredients in the order listed above. You should begin the machine by selecting the Wheat cycle with a 1 1/2-pound loaf, medium crust.

Nutrition Information

- Cal: 230
- Carbs:38.6 g
- Fat: 6.1 g
- Protein: 8.7 g
- Sodium: 259 mg

2. Bagel Gone Bananas

- Serving: 2
- Ready in: 5m

Ingredients

- Two tablespoons of natural nut butter, such cashew, almond, or peanut
- One teaspoon of honey
- A dash of salt
- One bagel with whole wheat, sliced and toasted
- One small banana, cut into slices

Direction

1. In a small bowl, mix salt, honey and nut butter together. Divide mixture on bagel halves. Put banana slices on top.

Nutrition Information

- Cal: 284
- Carbs:43 g
- Fat: 10 g
- Protein: 9 g

3. Banana Bread

- Serving: 16
- Prep: 15m
- Ready in: 1h15m

Ingredients

- All-purpose flour, one and a half cups
- Five grams of baking soda
- 250 g of white sugar and half a milligram of salt
- Two whisked eggs
- 1/4 cup butter, melted, three mashed bananas

Direction

1. Two 7 by 3-inch loaf pans should be buttered and floured. Set the oven's temperature to 175 degrees.
2. Mix the soda, salt, sugar, and flour together. Add the melted butter, lightly beaten eggs, and mashed bananas. To taste, you can add nuts. Put inside the pans.
3. Once the cake has baked for an hour at 175 degrees Celsius (350 degrees Fahrenheit), make sure a wooden toothpick placed in the center comes out clean.

Nutrition Information

- There are 145 calories.
- 26.5 g of Carb

- Protein: 2.3 g; Fat: 3.7 g
- 181 mg of sodium

4. Banana-blueberry Muffins

- Serving: 12
- Ready in: 1h

Ingredients

- Half a cup of low-fat or nonfat buttermilk
- Three quarter-cup of dense brown sugar
- Half a cup canola oil
- Two big eggs
- a cup of mashed, ripe bananas (about three medium)
- One and a half cups of whole-wheat pastry flour (see Note)
- All-purpose flour in 250 g
- Half a teaspoon raising agent
- one and a half teaspoons of ground cinnamon
- Half a tsp of baking powder
- ½ teaspoon each of nutmeg powder and salt
- 1/4 cup blueberries, either fresh or frozen

Direction

1. Start by preheating the oven to 400 degrees Fahrenheit. An optimal choice for baking muffins is to use a 12-muffin pan that is either lined with paper liners or coated with cooking spray.
2. Combine the eggs, oil, buttermilk, and brown sugar in a spacious basin. Incorporate the mashed bananas by stirring them.
3. Combine the nutmeg, salt, baking soda, cinnamon, rising agent, all-purpose flour, and whole-wheat pastry flour in a medium-sized basin.
4. Make sure to fully mix the dry and wet materials together.
5. Throw in some blueberries. Spoon the batter into each muffin cup until they are full.
6. Cook in an oven that has been heated beforehand for a duration of 20 to 25 minutes, or until the upper surface has acquired a golden brown color. A wooden skewer put into the center should emerge free of any residue.
7. Let it cool in the pan for ten minutes prior to taking it from the cups and cooling it on a wire rack for five minutes before serving.

Nutrition Information

- Cal: 232
- Carb: 41 grams
- Cholesterol: 31 milligrams

- The total amount of fat is 6 grams.
- 4 grams of protein

5. Banana-bran Muffins

- Serving: 12
- Ready in: 1h

Ingredients

- Two big eggs
- 2.3 quarts of thick brown sugar
- 250 g of ripe bananas mashed, two medium
- 250 g buttermilk; read the notes on ingredients
- 250 g of raw wheat bran; refer to the ingredient details.
- Canola oil, half a cup
- One-third cup of all-purpose flour and 250 g of whole-wheat flour
- one tsp vanilla extract
- Half a teaspoon raising agent
- Half a tsp of baking powder
- 1/4 tsp ground cinnamon
- A half-teaspoon of salt
- If preferred, use 1/2 cup chocolate chips.

Direction

1. Set the oven temperature to 400°F. Apply cooking spray to 12 muffin pans.
2. Combine eggs and brown sugar in a larger bowl and whisk until the mixture becomes smooth and creamy. Incorporate the oil, bananas, buttermilk, wheat bran, and vanilla by stirring.
3. Combine the whole-wheat flour, baking soda, cinnamon, salt, and rising agent in a large basin.
4. Verify that a dry component is prepared. Add the moist ingredients. Blend thoroughly with a rubber spatula.
5. Add the chocolate chips if you'd like. Muffin tins loaded with plenty of batter. Sprinkle with walnuts, if using.
6. Bake for 15 to 25 minutes, until the tops are lightly browned and the texture is slightly malleable.
7. Let the pan cool for five minutes. Let the edges loosen up. Place muffins onto a cooling rack. Before serving, let cool somewhat.

Nutrition Information

- Cal: 200
- Carbs:34 g
- Fat: 6 g

- Protein: 5 g

6. Banana-nut-chocolate Chip Quick Bread

- Serving: 12
- Ready in: 1h15m

Ingredients

- 1100 gs unbleached flour or unbleached pastry flour (see to the ingredient note).
- 250 g of flour for all purposes
- 1 and a half-tsp raising agent
- One tsp finely ground cinnamon
- Half a tsp of baking powder
- 1/4 teaspoon of nutmeg, ground
- A half-teaspoon of salt
- Two big eggs
- 250 g nonfat buttermilk; refer to the tip
- One-half cup brown sugar
- Two teaspoons of canola oil and two tablespoons of melted butter
- A tsp of vanilla extract
- two cups of chopped bananas
- 100 g finely chopped toasted walnuts , plus additional for garnish if preferred
- Half a cup of tiny chocolate chips

Direction

1. Set the oven temperature to 375°F for a large loaf or 400°F for little Bundts/muffins.
2. Apply a layer of cooking spray to the pans. Combine salt, nutmeg, baking soda, cinnamon, rising agent, all-purpose flour, and whole-wheat flour in a spacious basin.
3. Add eggs, vanilla, oil, butter, brown sugar, and buttermilk to another large dish and mix well.
4. Make a dry ingredient and stir wet ingredients just until incorporated.
5. Add walnuts, bananas, and chocolate chips; mix well. Pour batter into pans; optional walnut topping.
6. Place the small Bundts/muffins in the oven and bake them for a duration of 22 to 25 minutes. Check for doneness by inserting a skewer into the center of the baked goods. If the skewer comes out clean and the color is golden brown, they are ready.

7. Large loaves should be baked for a duration of 1 hour and 10 minutes, while tiny loaves require 35 minutes of baking time. Allow the pan to cool for a duration of 10 minutes.
8. Place on wire rack. Cool mini Bundts/muffins for 5 minutes, giant loaf for 35 minutes.
9. Pan choices:
10.   Large loaf, 9x5 pan.
11.   3-minute loaves—6x3-inch 2-cup pan.
12.   6-cup small Bundt pan for 6 little cakes, about 1 cup each.
13.   12, 2-1/2-inch muffin pan, regular 12-cup.

Nutrition Information

- Cal: 273 calories;
- Carbs:40 g
- Fat: 11 g
- Fiber: 3 g
- Protein: 6 g

7. Berry-almond Quick Bread

- Serving: 12
- Ready in: 1h15m

Ingredients

- One and a half cups whole-wheat flour or whole-wheat pastry flour (see note)
- 250 g of flour for all purposes
- 1½ tsps. raising agent
- One tsp finely ground cinnamon
- Half a tsp of baking powder
- A half-teaspoon of salt
- Two big eggs
- 250 g nonfat buttermilk; refer to the tip
- One-half cup brown sugar
- 35 g melted butter
- Double-thumb spread canola oil
- One teaspoon vanilla extract
- One-fourth teaspoon of extract from almonds
- Two cups of berries, either fresh or frozen (diced strawberries, blueberries, raspberries, and entire blackberries)
- 100 g finely chopped toasted sliced almonds , plus additional for garnish if preferred

Direction

1. Preheat the oven to 375 degrees Fahrenheit for large loaves and 400 degrees Fahrenheit for tiny loaves, bundts, and muffins. Coat cookware with cooking spray.
2. Combine the salt, baking soda, cinnamon, rising agent, all-purpose flour, and whole-wheat flour in a large bowl.
3. Combine the eggs, butter, oil, brown sugar, vanilla and almond extracts, and buttermilk in a spacious basin.
4. Create a depression in the dry ingredients. Thoroughly combine the wet components by stirring or blending. Incorporate the almonds and berries by mixing them together. Blend the ingredients together without excessive mixing. Transfer the batter into the pans. Optionally, garnish with almonds.
5. Once the dish is placed in the oven that has been prepared, a wooden skewer inserted into the center should emerge without any residue.
6. The baking time for little bundts or muffins is approximately 22-25 minutes, while mini loaves require about 35 minutes. Large loaves, on the other hand, need to be baked for approximately 1 hour and 10 minutes.
7. Place the pan(s) onto a wire rack and allow them to cool for a duration of 10 minutes.
8. Let the tiny loaves rest for a duration of thirty minutes, the large loaves for forty minutes, and the smaller bundts and muffins for a further five minutes.

Nutrition Information

- Cal: 221 calories;
- Carbs:33 g
- Fat: 7 g
- Fiber: 3 g
- Protein: 6 g

8. Bittersweet Pumpernickel Bread

- Serving: 12
- Prep: 30m
- Ready in: 3h25m

Ingredients

- one and a half cups heated water
- 2 tbsps. white vinegar
- 2 tsps. apple butter
- 2 tbsps. molasses
- 3 tbsps. brown sugar
- Three teaspoons of cocoa powder without sugar
- 1 tsp. ground coffee beans

- Half a teaspoon of salt
- Two tsp of melted butter
- One tablespoon of wheat germ
- Fennel seed, ½ teaspoon
- Two and a quarter tsp dry active yeast
- 1/4 kg flour (whole wheat) 4 ½ cup cooking spray for all-purpose flour
- 3 tablespoons cornmeal, split if necessary

Direction

1. In a stand mixer bowl with a dough hook, combine yeast, fennel seed, wheat germ, butter, salt, coffee, cocoa powder, brown sugar, molasses, apple butter, vinegar, and water.
2. Add the whole wheat flour and combine. After adding each cup of all-purpose flour, mix on medium-high speed.
3. Knead the dough for 4 minutes, until it is well combined and ball-shaped.
4. Coat a big basin with frying spray. Put the dough in a basin. Cover. The dough should have doubled in volume after one hour of rising in a warm environment.
5. Spread 1 tablespoon of cornmeal evenly over a large baking sheet.
6. Perform two divisions on the dough. Fold the edges of each dough ball underneath to form tightly packed loaves. Place the loaves on a baking sheet and bake them. Allow the dough to undergo a process of fermentation for a duration of one hour until it increases in size by a factor of two.
7. Set the oven temperature to 230°C / 450°F. Place a large pizza stone inside the oven.
8. Scatter 35 grams of cornmeal onto a bread paddle.
9. Delicately place a single loaf onto the bread paddle. Position the loaf gently on one side of the preheated pizza stone. Coat the bread paddle with the remaining cornmeal. Reallocate the second loaf once more.
10. Place in an oven that has been heated in advance and cook for a duration of five minutes. Reduce the oven temperature to 220°C/425°F.
11. Continue baking for an additional 30 minutes, or until the top has turned a golden brown color.
12. Place one bread paddle beneath each loaf. Proceed to the cutting board. Gently tap the bottom. Bread that sounds hollow is finished. Lay the loaves out obliquely. Allow a minimum of 20 minutes to cool.

Nutrition Information

- Cal: 262 calories;
- Carbs:52.3 g
- Fat: 2.9 g

9. Blueberry Corn Muffins

- Serving: 12
- Ready in: 40m

Ingredients

- A half of a cup of wholegrain flour
- 1/3 cup of all-purpose flour
- Half a cup of cornmeal
- One tablespoon raising agent
- One teaspoon ground cinnamon
- Half a teaspoon of salt
- 250 g of blueberries
- One big egg
- ⅔ cup nonfat milk
- Half a cup of honey
- Three tablespoons of canola oil
- One teaspoon of sugar

Direction

1. Adjust the oven temperature to 400°F. Apply cooking spray to 12 muffin tins with a diameter of 2 1/2 inches.
2. Combine the salt, cinnamon, raising agent, cornmeal, all-purpose flour, and whole wheat flour in a large basin. Incorporate blueberries. To apply a layer, mix thoroughly.
3. Whisk the eggs in a mixing bowl of moderate size. Thoroughly combine the milk, honey, and oil. Integrate the moist and arid constituents. Mix thoroughly. Refrain from excessive mixing. Transfer the batter into the prepared pan, ensuring that each cup is filled to a capacity of two-thirds. Add a little dusting of sugar to the surface.
4. After 18 to 22 minutes, carefully touch the muffin tops and they should spring back.
5. Cool the pan for five minutes. Allow the edges to loosen up. Place muffins on a wire cooling rack. Allow to cool before serving.

Nutrition Information

- Cal: 178
- Carbs:32 g
- Fat: 5 g
- Protein: 4 g

10.Blueberry-maple Muffins

- Serving: 12
- Ready in: 1h

Ingredients

- Whole flaxseeds, 1/4 cup
- 250 g + two teaspoons of whole-wheat flour.
- 1/4 tsp all-purpose flour. enhancing the representative
- One tsp finely ground cinnamon
- One-half teaspoon each of salt and baking soda
- Two big eggs
- 1/4 cup of pure maple syrup
- 250 g nonfat buttermilk; refer to the tip
- Half a cup canola oil
- One tablespoon orange juice and two tsp freshly grated orange zest
- One teaspoon vanilla extract
- One and a half-cup of raw blueberries
- One tablespoon of sugar

Direction

1. Adjust the oven temperature to 400 degrees. Apply cooking spray to twelve muffin pans.
2. Utilize a spice mill or a dry blender to pulverize the flaxseeds. Utilize a spacious receptacle.
3. Incorporate the whole wheat flour, cinnamon, baking soda, salt, and rising agent until thoroughly blended.
4. Blend the eggs and maple syrup together in a medium bowl until a smooth mixture is achieved. Incorporate the oil, zest, buttermilk, orange juice, and vanilla thoroughly.
5. Create a depression in the dry ingredients and incorporate the wet elements into them using a rubber spatula until they are thoroughly mixed. Incorporate the blueberries into the mixture by gently folding them in. Transfer the batter into the muffin tin. Add a small amount of sugar to the surface.
6. Place in a preheated oven and bake for 15 to 25 minutes, or until the tops achieve a golden brown color and regain their shape when gently pressed.
7. Let the pan cool for five minutes. After releasing the muffin's edges, let it cool on a wire rack.

Nutrition Information

- 209 calories
- 30 grams of Carb
- Eight grams of total fat

- 5 g of protein

11. Bread Machine Almond Bread

- 12 servings
- Prepare: ten meters
- Ready in: 3 minutes and 10 seconds

Ingredients

- 1. one-fourth cup water
- Four tablespoons of almond oil
- 1/4 cup honey, 1 cup almond flour, and 1 tsp salt
- two cups of flour made from whole wheat
- One-fourth cup of essential wheat gluten
- One teaspoon of xanthan gum
- One (.25 oz.) included dried yeast packet

Direction

1. Combine water, almond oil, salt, honey, almond flour, whole wheat flour, vital wheat gluten, xanthan gum, and yeast in the specified order within a bread maker.
2. To create a two-pound loaf, follow the directions on the package.

Nutrition Information

- Cal: 117
- Carbs:22 g
- Fat: 1.9 g
- Protein: 4.6 g

12. Bread Machine Ezekiel Bread

- Serving: 10
- Prep: 15m
- serves in: 3h30m

Ingredients

- A half-cup of milk
- A half cup of water.
- One egg.
- 1 tablespoon honey.
- 2 ½ tbsp olive oil split.
- 1 tablespoon of dried black beans.
- 1 tablespoon dried lentils

- 1 tablespoon dry kidney beans.
- 1 tablespoon barley.
- 1 cup of unbleached all-purpose flour.
- 1 cup flour made from whole wheat
- A quarter cup of millet flour
- One-half cup of rye flour
- Cracked wheat, a fourth of a
- 35 g of wheat germ.
- 1 teaspoon salt.
- 2 teaspoons bread machine yeast

Direction

1. In a microwave-safe glass measuring cup, combine water and milk and microwave for 35 seconds. Put the ingredients into the bread maker. Combine eggs, 35 g olive oil, and honey.
2. Using a coffee grinder, finely ground lentils, kidney beans, black beans, and barley.
3. Gather the grains, unbleached flour, millet flour, rye flour, cracked wheat, wheat germ, salt, and whole wheat flour in a bread machine. Put the yeast in next.
4. Choose the dough cycle for the bread machine.
5. When the bread maker begins to whistle, remove the dough and press it down.
6. Using the pastry towel, pinch the dough.
7. Use the leftover olive oil to coat a loaf pan. After shaping the dough into a loaf, transfer it to the pan. To achieve a twofold rise, cover with a damp towel and let it rise for forty minutes.
8. Set the oven temperature to 190°C, or 375°F.
9. Bake for 10 minutes without the dough cover.
10. Bake for 30–35 minutes, or until golden brown, at 175 degrees Celsius (350 degrees Fahrenheit).
11. After 10 minutes, remove the bread from the pan. Put aside to cool until you're ready to cut.

Nutrition Information

- Cal: 192
- Carbs:31.5 g
- Fat: 5 g
- Protein: 6.6 g

13. Bread Machine Honey-oat-wheat Bread

- Serving: 12
- Prep: 10m
- Ready in: 3h15m

Ingredients

- 2 ½ teaspoons dried active yeast
- Dozen tsp of white sugar
- One and a half cups of heated water (110°F/45°C)
- Three cups of all-purpose flour
- 250 g of flour made from whole wheat
- 250 g of rolled oats
- 3 tbsp of milk powder
- One teaspoon of salt
- 1/4 cup of honey
- one-fourth cup vegetable oil
- 3 tablespoons softened cooking spray and butter

Direction

1. Put the yeast, sugar, and water into a pan that you use to make bread.
2. Ten minutes after the yeast has come to a boil, let it dissolve. Put the rolled oats, whole wheat flour, powdered milk, salt, and all-purpose flour into a bowl and mix well.
3. Just keep being there. Incorporate the vegetable oil, butter, honey, and yeast into the mixture. Even out the flour mixture.
4. After choosing the Dough cycle, hit the "Start" button.
5. The bread machine cycle finishes after approximately 1.5 hours. In a 9 by 5 inch loaf pan that has been sprayed, transfer the dough. Just a warm spot for an hour will do the trick for the bread to rise.
6. A temperature of 190°C (375°F) should be used for the oven.
7. Bake for 35 minutes in a preheated oven, or until the top turns golden.

Nutrition Information

- Cal: 281 calories
- Carbs:44.7 g
- Fat: 8.9 g
- Protein: 6.4 g

14.Buttermilk Bread I

- Serving: 12

Ingredients

- 1 and Half a cup of buttermilk
- 1 1/2 tablespoon of margarine
- Two tsp white sugar
- One teaspoon of salt
- three cups of bread flour
- one and a third cups of whole wheat flour
- 15 g dry active yeast

Direction

1. Place the whole wheat flour, butter, margarine, sugar, yeast, and buttermilk in the bread machine pan in that sequence.
2. Choose the white bread baking option. Place on wire racks to cool down before slicing.

Nutrition Information

- Cal: 80
- Carbs:13.5 g
- Fat: 1.9 g
- Protein: 3.1 g

15.Buttermilk Whole Wheat Bread

- Serving: 12
- Prep: 15m
- Ready in: 2h50m

Ingredients

- 1 and Half a cup of buttermilk
- Three tablespoons of honey
- Two tablespoons of butter
- two and a third cups whole wheat flour
- 250 g of flour for all purposes
- essential wheat gluten (2) half a tablespoon
- Two tsp dry active yeast
- 2.5 g. lecithin powder
- A half-teaspoon of salt
- One pinch of ground ginger
- One sprinkle of powdered vitamin C cooking spray

Direction

1. In a microwave-safe bowl, mix butter, honey, and buttermilk. Heat each 30 seconds in the microwave until just under 43°C/110°F.
2. Put buttermilk in stand mixer bowl. Combine vitamin C powder, ginger, salt, lecithin, yeast, wheat gluten, all-purpose flour, and whole wheat flour. Low-speed mixing with a dough hook attachment until bowl sides are clean and dough just holds together. Rest dough 2 minutes in basin. Keep mixing for 2 minutes with dough hook.
3. Remove dough from bowl to work surface. Knead dough by hand for 2-3 minutes until elastic and hot.
4. Cooking spray a big basin. Turn dough in basin to butter both sides. Spray cooking spray on plastic wrap. Cover bowl spray-side down. Raise dough for an hour to double.
5. Fingerpress dough to deflate. Rise another 10-15 minutes.
6. Surface-turn dough. Roll into 8 1/2x11-inch rectangle. Squeeze seams and roll dough tightly from the short end. For a smooth top, fold ends under bread and squeeze edges.
7. Spray a loaf pan. Put loaf in pan. Wrap dough loosely in sprayed plastic. Let the dough rise 30-45 minutes to 1 1/2-2 in. above the pan.
8. Preheat the oven to 175°C/350°F. Remove loaf wrap.
9. Bake 35-40 minutes in preheated oven. Remove bread from pan with hot pads. Internal temperature should be 88°C/190°F. Cool loaf on wire rack. Slice.

Nutrition Information

- Cal: 173 calories;
- Carbs:31.6 g
- Fat: 3 g
- Protein: 6.6 g

16.Caramelized Onion & Goat Cheese Rolls

- Serving: 12
- Ready in: 45m

Ingredients

- 35 g extra virgin olive oil.
- 5 cups thinly chopped red onion.
- 35 g water.
- 1 teaspoon dried thyme
- A half teaspoon of salt
- 2.5 g ground pepper.

- 1. preferable whole wheat pizza dough
- Crumbled 4 ounces goat cheese

Direction

1. Get the oven hot, about 425 degrees Fahrenheit. Cooking spray a 12-cup muffin tin lightly.
2. One tablespoon of oil should be heated in a large skillet over medium-high heat. Onion should be part of it. Ten minutes with the cover on and stirring every so often.
3. Turn down the heat to medium-low. Salt, pepper, thyme, and water should be mixed together. If you want your vegetables to be soft and golden, simmer for 8 to 10 more minutes. To prevent browning too quickly, add water.
4. Using a floured board, flatten the dough into a rectangle that is 9 inches by 13 inches.
5. Empty the remaining tablespoon of oil. Scatter the onions over the dough. Goat cheese can be added.
6. Form the dough into a log shape by rolling it from longest side to shortest. Cut into 12 pieces. Prepare a muffin pan.
7. Brown the top by baking it for fifteen to twenty minutes. After 5 minutes, set aside to cool.

Nutrition Information

- Cal: 145
- Carbs:19 g
- Fat: 6 g
- Protein: 5 g

17.Chef John's Whole Wheat Ciabatta

- Serving: 12
- Prep: 45m
- Ready in: 18h15m

Ingredients

- Sponge:
- 250 g of hot water
- Half a cup of all-purpose flour
- Active dried yeast, one-fourth of a teaspoon, and half a cup of whole wheat flour and rye flour
- 250 g of flour for all purposes
- 1 cup of flour made from whole wheat
- 50 milliliters of water at ambient temperature

- 35 g of sunflower seeds to be shelled
- 1 teaspoon of polenta
- Flax seeds, ground, one tablespoon
- 1.75 teaspoons of salt
- a half teaspoon of honey
- 1 tablespoon of all-purpose flour, or more if necessary
- half a teaspoon of cornmeal, or water as required Water as required

Direction

1. A big mixing bowl is the perfect place to add yeast, 250 g of warm water, 1/4 cup of rye flour, 1/2 cup of whole wheat flour, 1/2 cup of all-purpose flour, and 250 g of rye flour.
2. Place plastic wrap around the basin. After five or six hours, the sponge should have inflated to twice its original size.
3. Stir together 250 grams of whole wheat flour and 250 grams of all-purpose flour in a sponge for three minutes with a wooden spoon. Add honey, salt, flax seeds, polenta, sunflower seeds, half a cup of water, and 250 grams of whole wheat flour. You want a sticky dough ball when you're done. Carefully rub the dish's sides. Cover the basin with plastic. After ten hours, the volume should have doubled.
4. Parchment should be used to line a baking sheet. On top, sprinkle some cornmeal and a half teaspoon of all-purpose flour.
5. Transfer the dough from the bowl to a lightly floured surface.
6. When you exhale, push down. A smooth, round loaf should be formed. Place the dough on a baking sheet that has been prepared.
7. Use flour to lightly dust the top of the loaf. Protect with a plastic wrap. Raise it for an hour and a half to double its size.
8. Preheating the oven to 230 degrees Celsius (450 degrees Fahrenheit) is mandatory. Put the baking dish on the lowest oven rack after filling it with water.
9. After the dough has risen, remove the plastic wrap. Drizzle some water over the dough.
10. Using water, mist the top of the loaf every 8 to 10 minutes, and bake the bread in an oven that has been warmed for 30 to 35 minutes, until it is hollow and brown. Organize the bread on the cooling rack. After it has cooled, slice.

Nutrition Information

- Cal: 135
- Carbs:26.6 g
- Fat: 1.6 g
- Protein: 4.5 g

18. Cherry-berry Banana Bread

- Serving: 16
- Prep: 20m
- Ready in: 55m

Ingredients

- 250 g of all-purpose flour
- 100 g of whole-wheat flour
- Half a cup of regular rolled oats
- A single tsp of baking soda
- One tsp finely ground cinnamon
- One-third teaspoon kosher salt
- Half a cup of melted butter
- 100 g sugar
- One 6-oz jar of nonfat plain Greek yogurt
- ¾ cup thawed, chilled or frozen egg product
- 1/2 cup of mashed ripe bananas
- Half a cup nonfat milk
- One teaspoon of vanilla
- 1100 g cherry berry blend frozen fruit

Direction

1. Turn the oven on high heat (350°F). Gently coat eight small loaf pans with spray.
2. Set aside the pan bottoms and line them with wax or parchment paper. Gather the flours, cinnamon, oats, baking soda, and kosher salt in a sizable basin.
3. The butter should be beaten for 30 seconds at medium to high speed in a medium basin using an electric mixer.
4. Mix in the sugar gradually. Scrub the edges of the bowl. Incorporate another two minutes of beating. Add the yogurt, banana, egg, milk, and vanilla. Mix through.
5. Without delay, combine the flour and banana mixture. Blend until combined. Shrink the enormous frozen fruit pieces. Reserve a quarter cup of the fruit. Include any unused fruit in the batter. In each loaf pan, pour 3/4 cup batter. Place the leftover fruit on top of the loaves.
6. If you insert a wooden toothpick near the middle and wait 30–35 minutes, it should come out clean. Allow the pans to cool on a wire rack for five minutes.
7. Remove the skillets. On wire racks, it works wonderfully. Wash the bottoms of the loaves to remove the paper.

Nutrition Information

- Cal: 135
- Carbs:22 g
- Fat: 3 g
- Protein: 4 g

19. Chive & Garlic Breadsticks

- Serving: 16
- Ready in: 45m

Ingredients

- 1 pound of pizza dough, ideally whole-wheat
- half a tablespoon of extra-virgin olive oil
- 3 tbsps. dried chives
- 3 g. garlic powder

Direction

1. Position racks in the oven's upper and bottom thirds. Preheat the oven to 400° Fahrenheit.
2. Line two baking trays with either cooking spray or parchment paper.
3. Divide the dough in sixteen equal pieces. On a lightly floured board, roll each into a 12- to 14-inch breadstick. Breadsticks should be at least 1/2 inch apart on baking pans.
4. Spread a thin layer of oil. Press in the garlic powder and chives, if necessary.
5. Breadsticks should be gently browned in 15-20 minutes on lower and upper racks, changing pans halfway through. Transfer to wire racks. Cool.

Nutrition Information

- Cal: 74
- Carbs:11 g
- Fat: 3 g
- Protein: 2 g

20. Clare's Whole Wheat Potato Bread

- 24 servings
- Prepare: twenty-five meters
- Ready in three hours

Ingredients

- Two cups of all-purpose flour
- A measure of 1.5 cups of pre-mashed potatoes
- Two and a half teaspoons of salt

- Two packages (.25 oz) of active dry yeast
- one and a half cups heated water
- 1 1/4 cup heated milk
- one-fourth cup margarine
- 1/4 cup honey and two beaten eggs
- 2. half a cup of flour made from whole wheat

Direction

1. Mix yeast, salt, potato flakes, and all-purpose flour in a large basin. In another dish, mix eggs, honey, margarine, milk, and water. Beat liquid into dry ingredients. Slowly add whole wheat flour until evenly saturated. Knead for 5 minutes. Put in oiled basin. Cover with a clean kitchen towel. Wait an hour for the dough to double in bulk.
2. Two 5x9-inch loaf pans greased. Dough punchdown. Form loaves. Put in pans. Let it rise in pans for 1 hour.
3. Heat the oven to 190°C/375°F. After 35 minutes, loaves should be hollow and light golden.

Nutrition Information

- Cal: 132 calories;
- Carbs:23.2 g
- Fat: 2.9 g
- Protein: 4.2 g

21.Coconut-carrot Morning Glory Muffins

- Serving: 12
- Ready in: 1h

Ingredients

- 250 g of either white or whole-wheat flour
- 100 g of traditional rolled oats and two tablespoons of garnish
- Two teaspoons raising agent
- Two tsp of cinnamon powder
- Half a teaspoon of salt
- ¼ tsp. ground allspice
- 2 large eggs
- 250 g of plain applesauce
- One-half cup honey
- Two tsp of vanilla essence
- One-fourth cup of melted coconut oil
- two cups of carrots, shredded
- 100 g of shredded coconut without sugar and two tablespoons as a garnish

- 1/2 cup of raisins

Direction

1. Turn the oven on high heat (350°F). Apply cooking spray to a muffin tray with 12 cups.
2. Stir together the whole wheat flour, half a cup of oats, cinnamon, salt, and allspice in a medium bowl.
3. Combine the applesauce, eggs, honey, and vanilla in a big basin and whisk to combine. Add a small amount of coconut oil. Stir in the flour mixture gradually to incorporate. Add the carrots, raisins, and half of the coconut. Mix well.
4. Pour batter into each muffin cup. Add the final 35 g of coconut and oats.
5. Bake for 35 to 35 minutes, or until a toothpick inserted in the center comes out with moist crumbs and comes out gently. Ten minutes should pass in the pan. Place atop a wire rack. Servings should be at room temperature or slightly warm.

Nutrition Information

- Cal: 186
- Carbs:28 g
- Fat: 8 g
- Protein: 4 g

22.Cracked Wheat Bread 1

- Serving: 12
- Prep: 5m
- Ready in: 3h5m

Ingredients

- one and a quarter cups water
- Two tablespoons softened margarine
- Two tablespoons powdered milk
- Two tsp brown sugar
- 1 1/4 teaspoon salt
- three cups of flour for bread
- 1/3 cup of flour made from whole wheat
- quarter of a cup cracked wheat
- one and One-fourth teaspoon dried active yeast

Direction

1. Follow the manufacturer's instructions for measuring the ingredients in the bread machine pan.

2. After choosing the standard or light cycle, hit the start button.

Nutrition Information

- Cal: 50
- Carbs:7.3 g
- Fat: 1.9 g
- Protein: 1.4 g

23.Cracked Wheat Bread II

- Serving: 20
- Prep: 20m
- Ready in: 55m

Ingredients

- one and a quarter cups heated water
- half a cup of cereal with cracks
- One package (.25 oz) of active dry yeast
- One-third cup of heated water (110°F/45°C)
- 2 tbsps. butter, softened
- 3 g. salt
- 2 tbsps. molasses
- 2 tbsps. honey
- 250 g of milk
- 250 g of flour made from whole wheat
- Four cups of all-purpose flour

Direction

1. An insignificant saucepan brings water to a boil. Include cracked wheat. Low heat for ten minutes. A smidgen of coolness.
2. In a small basin of hot water, dissolve the yeast. It will get creamy after 10 minutes.
3. A big basin should be filled with cracked wheat. Bring the yeast mixture to a boil and add 2 cups of bread flour, whole wheat flour, honey, butter, molasses, and milk.
4. Mix in the rest of the flour, half a cup at a time, beating after each addition.
5. After the dough has combined, transfer it to a board that has been lightly dusted with flour. Make sure the dough is elastic and smooth by kneading it for 10 minutes.
6. Pour oil into a large bowl. Place the bowl over the dough. Get to the oil on your map. Use a damp cloth to cover. After being exposed to heat for one hour, its volume ought to have quadrupled.

7. Make the dough less pliable. Place on a floured surface and transfer. Divide the dough into two equal halves so you can shape the loaves.
8. Grease two loaf pans that measure 9 by 5 inches. Use a moist towel to cover the bread. The volume will quadruple after 40 minutes. At the same time, get the oven up to 190°C, or 375°F.
9. Preheat the oven to 375 degrees. When tapped on both the top and bottom, the bread should sound hollow. This should be done after 30 to 35 minutes in the oven. Cool the items on a rack.

Nutrition Information

- Cal: 151
- Carbs:29.5 g
- Fat: 1.8 g
- Protein: 4.4 g

24. Cracked Wheat Sourdough Bread

- Serving: 24

Ingredients

- 3/4 cup of cracked wheat
- A single cup of hot water
- 25% margarine, melted, 1/4 cup
- 2 tbsps. molasses
- 2 tbsps. honey
- 3/4 cup nonfat milk
- A quarter cup of flaxseed—
- One-half cup raw sunflower seeds
- two and a half cups sourdough starter
- two cups of flour made from whole wheat
- 3. half a cup of flour for bread
- One beaten egg

Direction

1. Fill a medium basin with hot, but not boiling, water to cover the broken wheat. Stir in molasses, honey, sunflower, flax, and nonfat milk. Mix well. Warm up a bit. Mix in the sourdough starter.
2. Start adding 1 cup of flour at a time, first whole wheat and then bread flour, using a large wooden spoon. Once the dough is manageable, transfer it onto a surface dusted with flour. Knead for 10 to 12 minutes, using as little of the residual flour as possible.
3. Roll the elastic, smooth dough into a ball and transfer to an oiled bowl. Turn and brush the sides with the coating. Keep covered and in a draft-free, warm

place. Allow to rise until bulk doubles, about 1 and a half hours. Gently press down on the rising dough. Move back to a warm place and allow to rise for one further hour, or until doubled.

4. Punch down the dough once it has risen for one more time. Go ahead and bake two loaves of bread. Before sealing, press the dough into two 9x5 loaf pans. After an hour of rising, the dough should have multiplied by two and be at least an inch above the pan's edge. To produce the egg wash, whisk the whole egg with a tablespoon of water. Top the loaves with the beaten egg.

5. Heat the oven to 190°C (375°F). Rotate the pans and spray them with cold water quickly after 15 minutes of baking. Set the oven timer for 30 minutes. Loaves are done baking when they return their shapes when touched on both the top and bottom. Wait 10 minutes for the pans to cool on the racks. Face the shelves. Incredible, in a word.

Nutrition Information

- Cal: 200 calories
- Carbs:36.1 g
- Fat: 3.9 g
- Protein: 7.4 g

25.Cranberry Nut Whole Wheat Yeast Bread

- 10 servings
- Prepare: ten meters
- Ready in: thirty-two minutes

Ingredients

- Three-thirds cup white whole wheat flour
- 1.5/3 cups of hot water
- 1/3 cup agave syrup
- 3 tbsps. vegetable oil
- 2 tbsps. ground flax seeds
- 4 tsps. vital wheat gluten
- 3 g. yeast
- 1 tsp. salt
- 1/3 cup dried cranberries
- 3 tbsps. chopped toasted hazelnuts
- 2 tbsps. finely chopped almonds
- 2 tbsps. chopped pistachio nuts

Direction

1. Following the manufacturer's instructions, add salt, yeast, essential wheat gluten, flax seeds, oil, agave syrup, water, and white whole wheat flour to a

bread machine. Do the dough cycle. Add pistachios, almonds, hazelnuts, and cranberries in the second kneading.

2. Grease an 8x4 loaf pan. Get the dough from the machine. Punch lightly. Form a loaf. Put in pan. Cover. Let rise 45 minutes until nearly doubled.
3. Heat the oven to 175°C/350°F.
4. The loaf top should be golden brown after 40 minutes in a preheated oven.

Nutrition Information

- Cal: 287
- Carbs:46.5 g
- Fat: 9.5 g
- Protein: 8 g

26.Cranberry-pecan Cinnamon Rolls

- Serving: 12
- Ready in: 1h

Ingredients

- 3 tbsps. butter, melted
- One-fourth cup of dark brown sugar
- 1/4 cup either light corn syrup or brown rice syrup
- Chopped fresh cranberries, 250 g
- ⅛ cup of pecans, chopped
- Divide 1½ tsp ground cinnamon into 1 cup white whole-wheat flour .
- 250 g of flour for all purposes
- Two tablespoons of powdered sugar
- One tablespoon raising agent
- ½ teaspoon each of salt and baking soda
- Two tablespoons of chilled butter, sliced
- 1 cup cold buttermilk
- 2 tbsps. canola oil

Direction

1. Bake at 375 degrees Fahrenheit until golden brown. Apply cooking spray to a muffin tray with 12 cups.
2. Combine 1 teaspoon of cinnamon, pecans, cranberries, brown sugar, corn syrup, and melted butter in a small bowl. Each muffin pan should have a tablespoon of batter in the bottom.
3. Gather the remaining 2.5 grams of cinnamon, baking soda, salt, granulated sugar, rising agent, all-purpose flour, and whole wheat flour in a large mixing basin. Add the sugar and stir well. Pour in the cooled butter.

4. Cut the butter into pea-sized pieces with two knives or your fingertips. Drizzle with oil and buttermilk. Just mix everything together. Pour batter into cranberry mixture; around 35 g should be used per person.
5. Bake rolls till edges brown softly, 18–20 minutes. Pan-cool for 10 minutes. Knife-loosen edges of each. Place a large serving tray over the pan. Invert rolls on it. Top rolls with pan leftover topping. Warm serve.

Nutrition Information

- Cal: 220
- Carbs:31 g
- Fat: 10 g
- Protein: 3 g

27.Cream Cheese And Almond Wheat Bread

- 10 servings
- Prepare: 20 minutes
- Prepared in: 2 hours and 45 minutes

Ingredients

- 250 g of hot water
- 2 tbsps. brown sugar
- One package (25 oz) of active dry yeast
- 250 g of whipped cream cheese
- half a cup of almonds, chopped
- Three tablespoons of milk
- Two tablespoons vegetable oil
- Two tablespoons of honey
- One tablespoon of salt
- 1/2 cup of flour for all purposes
- one and a half cups flour made from whole wheat

Direction

1. Warm the water and mix in the yeast, brown sugar, and brown sugar in a big basin.
2. Allow five minutes for the yeast to soften and make a creamy foam. Grease the second large basin. Put aside.
3. Combine yeast, milk, almonds, honey, vegetable oil, and whipped cream cheese. Place in the blender. Blend until smooth.
4. Cream cheese and all-purpose flour should be whisked together slowly in a big mixing bowl. Flour made from whole wheat is one example. Mix until a smooth dough forms.

5. After flouring the board, turn the dough over. After about 8 minutes of kneading, the dough should be smooth and springy.
6. Coat a bowl with oil and add the dough. Once you turn the dough over, oil the top. Cover the dish with a cloth. To make double dough, let it rest for 45 minutes.
7. Turn the oven on high heat (350°F, 175°C). Press some butter into a loaf pan that measures 5 by 9 inches.
8. Tap the dough to flatten it. Flour a board and knead the dough once more.
9. Bake a single loaf. Scoop the dough into a lightly greased loaf pan. After 45 minutes in a warm place, the dough should have doubled in size.
10. Fifty to sixty minutes in the oven should be enough time for the bread to brown on top and be done in the middle.
11. Use aluminum foil to prevent the bread from turning black while cooking.

Nutrition Information

- Cal: 272 calories
- Carbs:36.2 g
- Fat: 12 g
- Protein: 7.2 g

28.Dee's Health Bread

- Serving: 72

Ingredients

- Two tbsp dry active yeast
- One teaspoon of white sugar
- half a cup of hot water
- 3. half a cup heated water
- 1/4 cup molasses and 1/4 cup honey
- one-half cup of vegetable oil
- two eggs
- Two tsp lemon juice
- Seven cups of whole wheat flour
- one-fourth cup flaxseed
- one-fourth cup of cracked wheat
- one-fourth cup of sunflower seeds
- Four teaspoons of salt
- four cups of flour for bread

Direction

1. Dissolve the sugar and yeast in half a cup of warm water in a small bowl.

2. It is recommended to combine the eggs, oil, molasses, honey, lemon juice, and the remaining 3 ½ cups of warm water in a large bowl.
3. Be sure to mix thoroughly. Get the yeast mixture stirred.
4. Incorporate 5 cups of whole wheat flour gradually while vigorously beating after each addition.
5. Mix together the sunflower seeds, cracked wheat, and flax. Give it a good stir.
6. After the mixture becomes light, wait for twenty minutes. Mix in the salt and the rest of the flours until a dough forms that pulls away from the sides of the bowl.
7. Roll out and smooth the dough by kneading it for ten to fifteen minutes. Spoon into a basin that has been pre-oiled. Shut up. Turn the oven light on and let it rise for an hour, or until doubled in size.
8. Bring it down to a punch. Shape into six spheres and place a lid on each. Tend to them for a while.
9. Put together loaves. Bake, covered, until the mixture has doubled in size. The recommended baking time is 25–35 minutes at a temperature of 190°C (375°F).

Nutrition Information

- Cal: 94
- Carbs:16.6 g
- Fat: 2.2 g
- Protein: 3 g

29. Double Chocolate-banana Bread Pudding

- Serving: 12
- Ready in: 2h

Ingredients

- 5 big eggs
- 3 big egg whites
- 35 oz of whole milk
- Half a cup of light brown sugar
- 100 g chocolate powder, unsweetened
- 100 g chocolate chips, semisweet
- 3 g. vanilla extract
- ¼ tsp. salt
- two cups of ripe bananas chopped
- Eight cups of day-old, ½-inch whole-wheat bread cubes
- 100 g finely chopped, roasted salted peanuts

Direction

1. In a large mixing bowl, combine egg whites and eggs. Combine salt, vanilla extract, chocolate chips, cocoa powder, brown sugar, and milk.
2. Add banana. Mix until well blended. Put bread. Combine. Be patient for thirty minutes.
3. To absorb custard, push the bread into the liquid many times.
4. Bring the oven temperature up to 350 degrees Fahrenheit. Apply cooking spray to a shallow baking dish that holds 3 quarts of liquid.
5. Fill the pan with pudding. Apply cooking spray to the foil. Put the sprayed side down on top of the pan.
6. After 30 minutes of baking, uncover. Distribute the peanuts.
7. Continue to bake for another 25 to 30 minutes, or until firm and puffy. Let it cool for 15 minutes before serving.

Nutrition Information

- 300 calories
- 46 g of Carb
- 9 g of total fat
- 12 g of protein

30. Easy Whole Wheat Bread

- Serving: 12
- Prep: 10m
- Ready in: 3h10m

Ingredients

- One and a half cups warm water (110°F/45°C)
- 3 g. powdered egg substitute (optional)
- 2 tbsps. vegetable oil
- 2 tbsps. sugar
- 1 tsp. salt
- 250 g of flour for bread
- 250 g of flour made from whole wheat
- 1 tsp. rapid rise yeast

Direction

1. Melt the egg substitute in warm water.
2. Add each ingredient to the bread maker pan according to the handbook's directions.
3. Set the machine's bake time to normal and start the whole wheat cycle.

4. Check how the dough is kneading after five minutes. Depending on the consistency, one tablespoon flour or water may be needed. Once the bread has cooled on a wire rack, slice it.

Nutrition Information

- Cal: 65
- Carbs:9.6 g
- Fat: 2.5 g
- Protein: 1.7 g

31.Elaine's Cracked Wheat Bread

- Serving: 20
- Prep: 25m
- Ready in: 3h10m

Ingredients

- 1. half a cup water
- half a cup of cereal with cracks
- half a cup of hot water
- One tablespoon of white sugar and one tablespoon of salt
- Just one tablespoon of yeast
- 250 g of buttermilk
- half a cup of honey
- One-fourth cup molasses
- 1/4 cup of butter
- one-fourth cup wheat germ
- One-fourth cup of flax seeds
- One-fourth cup milled bran
- two cups of flour made from whole wheat
- Four cups of all-purpose flour
- 35 g melted butter

Direction

1. In a saucepan, combine salt, cracker wheat, and 1/2 cup water. Boil. Cool to medium-low. Cook, stirring occasionally, for 15 minutes to absorb water. Get away from the heat.
2. In a large bowl, combine the yeast, sugar, and 1/3 cup water. Leave the yeast for 5 minutes to produce creamy foam.
3. Combine broken wheat, bran, flaxseed, wheat germ, 1/4 cup butter, molasses, honey, and buttermilk. Include whole wheat flour.

4. Using a spoon or an electric mixer, stir the broken wheat into the yeast mixture. Slowly add 1 cup all-purpose flour and whisk until the dough is elastic and smooth.
5. Grease a big bowl and add the dough. Cover. Wait one hour for it to double.
6. Deflate the dough by punching it. Cut the dough in half evenly. Roll the pieces into rectangles to remove air bubbles. Pinch the seams and tuck the sides as you roll it.
7. Grease two 9 by 5 loaf pans. Roll seam side down in pans. Press to flatten. Top-tuck all corners using your finger.
8. Cover. After 45 minutes of rising in a warm environment, the dough should be an inch above the rim of the pan.
9. Preheat the oven to 190°C (375°F).
10. Bake the loaves for 35 minutes, until golden brown and hollow when tapped. Use 2 tablespoons of melted butter. Place them on wire racks. Cool. Slice it after chilling.

Nutrition Information

- Cal: 236
- Carbs:43.2 g
- Fat: 5.1 g
- Protein: 6.1 g

32. Essene Bread For The Bread Machine

- Serving: 15
- Prep: 1h30m
- Ready in: 3days11h20m

Ingredients

- Half a cup of ground sprouted wheat berries
- A cup buttermilk
- One egg
- 35 g maple syrup
- Half a teaspoon of salt
- ½ teaspoon baking soda
- Vital wheat gluten, 35 g
- 2. one-fourth cup of whole wheat flour
- One and a half tsp dry active yeast

Direction

1. Try washing and draining 1/2 cup fresh wheat berries in lukewarm water a few days ahead of time before making this bread. Soak the cleaned berries in lukewarm water in a large basin. The berries should be covered with a cloth

or plate and let to soak for 12 hours or overnight at room temperature. Berries are quite good at absorbing moisture. To prevent the soaked berries from drying out, rinse them in a sieve and cover them with a plate in a dark spot. Try washing the berries three times a day to keep an eye out for sprouts. The sprouts will reach a maximum length of 1/4 inch in a few days. Use a food processor or blender to mash the berry sprouts once they have been drained.

2. In the bread machine pan, arrange the ingredients in the manufacturer's recommended order. Press the Start button after choosing Medium Crust and Whole Wheat.
3. To preserve sprouts, place them in the bread machine's Raisin cycle at the signal. The bread may be pulpy without a Raisin cycle in the bread maker.

Nutrition Information

- Cal: 104 calories.
- Carbs:20.6 g
- Fat: 0.9 g
- Protein: 4.9 g

33. Everyday Whole-wheat Bread

- Serving: 14
- Ready in: 1day

Ingredients

- ¼ cup broken wheat, often known as bulgur
- Half a cup of boiling water
- Measure out 2100 gs plus 1 tablespoon of whole-wheat flour, divide 1100 gs of unbleached bread flour (per the note), add extra if needed, and toast 35 g of wheat germ (optional).
- 1 1/4 tsp. table salt
- One-fourth teaspoon instant, quick-rising, or bread machine yeast
- a half-cup of ice water , plus additional as needed
- ¼ cup honey, like honey from clover or any other mild type
- Three tablespoons of tasteless vegetable oil, such as canola or maize oil.

Direction

1. Dough: Mix broken wheat/bulgur and hot water in a medium bowl. Add yeast, salt, wheat germ (optional), 1 3/4 cups bread flour, and 2 1/2 cups whole-wheat flour to a 4-quart basin and stir well. Oil, honey, and 1 3/4 cups icy water should be well mixed with bulgur. Scrape sides and vigorously mix wet and dry ingredients until dough is fully combined. The dough should be firm, sticky, and wet. If mixture is dry, add just enough cold water to combine, not

too much. If dough is too moist, add enough bread flour to firm it. Lightly oil top. Wrap the bowl in plastic.

2. **Initial rise:** Let dough rise at room temperature for 12-18 hours (70°F). If convenient, mix halfway through rising. Refrigerate dough for 3-12 hours before initial rise for taste and convenience.

3. Oil a 9x5-inch loaf pan or big pan for the second rise. Forceful stirring deflates dough. Add bread flour to soft dough to make it stiff, moist, and hard to combine. Put dough in pan. Lightly oil top. Use fingertips/well-oiled rubber spatula to smooth and press dough into pan. Top with leftover 3 g. whole wheat flour and smooth with fingertips. Top with the remainder 3 g. whole-wheat flour and smooth with your hands. Cut a 1/2-inch deep loaf slit with a serrated knife/well-oiled kitchen shears. Wrap the pan in plastic.

4. Raise dough at warm room temperature for 1–2 1/2 hours until plastic. Gently remove plastic. Depending on temperature, dough should rise one inch above the pan rim in 15–45 minutes.

5. Place rack in lower third of oven 20 minutes before baking. Set oven temperature to 375°F.

6. Bake, let cool, then cut. Bake loaf on lower rack for 55–65 minutes, or until golden. Use foil to shield. Bake for a further 10 to 15 minutes, or until a skewer inserted in the center comes out covered in crumbs and an instant-read thermometer reads 204 to 206°. Cool the pan for ten to fifteen minutes on a wire rack. On the rack, turn the loaf. Before serving, reheat. It is better to eat cold bread slices than warm ones.

Nutrition Information

- Cal: 188 calories.
- Carbs:35 g
- Fat: 4 g
- Protein: 5 g

34.Fabulous Homemade Bread

- Serving: 72

Ingredients

- half a cup of hot water
- Three packages of active dry yeast (.25 oz.)
- one-fourth cup bread flour
- One tablespoon of white sugar
- Two cups of instant oats
- two cups of flour made from whole wheat

- 4 half a cup heated water
- 1 1/35 g of salt
- two and a third cups brown sugar
- two and a third cups of vegetable oil
- ten cups of bread flour

Direction

1. In the bowl of an electric mixer, combine 1/4 cup of bread flour, 1 tablespoon of sugar, and 1/2 cup of warm water with the yeast. Wait half an hour for it to set. Rapid effervescence occurred.
2. Mix the oats, 2/3 cup sugar, 2/3 cup oil, salt, 4 1/2 cups warm water, and whole wheat flour in a bowl.
3. Stir the dough for a minute or two on low speed with the dough hooks. Quicken the pace a little.
4. To make sure the dough pulls away from the bowl, add bread flour 1/2 cup to 1 cup at a time.
5. Depending on the relative humidity, the amount of flour needed to prevent the bread from pulling away from the edges of the bowl could vary. Floury dough is acceptable.
6. Preheat a bowl and transfer the dough to it. Move on to the outerwear. Use a damp cloth to cover. Allow it to grow to twice its original size in a warm place for one hour.
7. Six equal halves of dough should be divided. Make loafs. Transfer to oiled 8x4 pans. After an hour, the dough should be about an inch above the pan's rim.
8. Bake tops at 175°C/350°F for 35 minutes, or until browned. Give the pans ten minutes to cool. Turn to face the wire racks. Wonderful beyond words.

Nutrition Information

- 44 calories and 5.5 grams of Carb
- Protein: 0.9 g and Fat: 2.3 g

35.Flax And Sunflower Seed Bread

- Serving: 15
- Prep: 10m
- Ready in: 3h

Ingredients

- one and a third cups of water
- Two tablespoons softened butter
- Three tablespoons of honey
- One and a half cups of bread flour
- One and a third cup of whole wheat flour for baking

- One teaspoon of salt
- 1 teaspoon dried active yeast
- The amount of flax seeds and sunflower seeds needed is half a cup each.

Direction

1. In the bread machine pan, add all the ingredients (apart from the sunflower seeds) following the manufacturer-recommended order.
2. Go ahead and start the usual white cycle. Add the sunflower seeds when the machine beeps to indicate that kneading is about to occur.

Nutrition Information

- Cal: 140 calories
- Carbs:22.7 g
- Fat: 4.2 g

36.Good 100% Whole Wheat Bread

- Serving: 12
- Prep: 5m
- Ready in: 3h5m

Ingredients

- dried active yeast, 1 and 1/2 tablespoons
- three cups of flour made from whole wheat
- one and aHalf a teaspoon of salt
- one and a half tablespoons refined sugar
- 1 1/35 g powdered nonfat dry milk
- 1 and 1/2 tablespoons of butter
- One and a quarter cups warm water (110°F/45°C)

Direction

1. The manufacturer's recommended order of ingredients should be followed when adding them to the bread machine pan.
2. Either choose Whole Wheat or Basic Bread. Turn on your computer.

Nutrition Information

- Cal: 124 calories.
- Carbs:24 g
- Fat: 1.9 g
- Protein: 4.7 g

37.Grandma Cornish's Whole Wheat Potato Bread

- Serving: 48

Ingredients

- 1 medium-sized peeled potato
- two cups of water
- One teaspoon of salt
- one-third cup of white sugar
- one-third cup shortening
- 3 g. salt
- Six warm milk cups
- Three packages of active dry yeast (.25 oz.)
- One-half cup of heated water (110°F/45°C)
- One teaspoon of white sugar
- Fifteen cups of whole wheat flour

Direction

1. Melt the yeast in 1/2 cup warm water with 1 tsp sugar.
2. In two cups of water, boil one teaspoon salt and a medium-peeled potato. Mash the potato in a medium-sized basin, being careful to retain the water. In a big bowl, combine milk, mashed potato, oil or shortening, 1 tablespoon salt, 1/3 cup sugar, and potato water.
3. Add yeast to the heated milk mixture. Add 15 cups of whole wheat flour and stir.
4. On a slightly floured surface, turn the dough. For ten minutes, knead. Place in a basin that is oiled. To coat, turn. Use a damp cloth to cover. It will double in 1 1/2 hours. Take it down. Again, knead for three minutes. Let's get back to bowling. Allow to rise once more until doubled. Punch down following your two-hour ascent. Form four loaves. Butter two 9 x 5 bread pans. For another 30 to 60 minutes, let the dough rise.
5. Bake for 1 hour at 165°C/325°F.

Nutrition Information

- Cal: 165 calories;
- Carbs:31.1 g
- Fat: 2.7 g
- Protein: 6.4 g

38.Herbed Potato Bread

- Serving: 16
- Ready in: 3h30m

Ingredients

- Bread
- One 6-ounce all-purpose potato, peeled and cut in half
- One tablespoon of extra virgin olive oil
- Two tablespoons of warm water and half a teaspoon of sugar
- One-half tsp dried active yeast
- one and a half cups unbleached flour
- One tablespoon of just-picked rosemary
- 1 tablespoon of just-picked thyme
- 1 tsp finely cut sage
- 1/4 tsp salt
- 1½–1¾ cups flour for all purposes
- Using cornmeal to dust
- Apply glaze and embellish.
- Six new chives
- 6–8 fresh flat-leaf parsley sprigs
- 4–6 new leaves of sage
- One white egg
- One tablespoon of water

Direction

1. Put the potato and water in a small saucepan and heat until it boils. Switch to medium-low heat. After tender, cook for 15 to 20 minutes under cover; drain. Save 1 cup of the cooking liquid. Use a fork to mash the potato in a bowl. Drizzle with oil. After mashing the potatoes, reserve the hot, boiling liquid.
2. Dissolve the sugar in the water in a big basin. Whisk in the yeast. To make foam, wait five minutes. Mash the potato with any excess hot water. A little at a time, beat in the whole wheat flour. Temporarily, pause. Add the rosemary, thyme, sage, and salt, and mix well. To make the dough too stiff to whip, gradually add small amounts of all-purpose flour while stirring constantly. After flouring the surface, transfer the dough there. Knead for approximately 10 minutes, or until elastic and smooth, adding flour to avoid sticking. Mixing and kneading dough is a breeze with a stand-up mixer and a dough hook.
3. Line a basin with a thin layer of oil. Next, put on a coat. Use plastic wrap to protect. Let rise for 1 1/2 hours or until the volume doubles.
4. Apply cooking spray on a sizable baking sheet. Dust with cornmeal. Dough is punched down. Work the dough a few times on a surface. half-baked. Form

each into a ball. Place your loves a few inches apart on a baking sheet. Use plastic wrap to protect. Give yourself an hour to get up.

5. Half an hour before baking, place a stone or baking sheet upside down on the middle rack of the oven. Put a little baking pan underneath. Aim for 450°F in the oven.

6. adorning bread: Set up a big bowl of ice water next to the flames. Raise a big pot to a boil. Sage, parsley, and chives should be briefly submerged in boiling water. Use tongs or a slotted spoon to retrieve. Add chilly water. Dry-brush the herbs.

7. In a little dish, combine the egg white and water with a fork. Brush the risen loaves. Arrange sprigs of herbs to adorn loaves. Again, brush with egg-white glaze.

8. Fill the oven baking pan with 250 g of water. Lay baking sheet over inverted baking sheet or stone. Bread is baked for twenty minutes. Preheat the oven to 400°. Bake loaves for ten to fifteen minutes, or until the bottoms are brown and hollow to the touch. On a wire rack, cool.

Nutrition Information

- Cal: 113 calories
- Carbs:22 g
- Fat: 1 g
- Fiber: 2 g
- Protein: 4 g

39. High Fiber Bread

- Serving: 24
- Prep: 10m
- Ready in: 2h30m

Ingredients

- One and a third cups heated water
- Four tablespoons of molasses
- 1 tablespoon dried active yeast
- Two and a half cups whole wheat flour
- A cup of ground flaxseed
- 2/3 cup of bread flour
- Half a cup of oat bran
- one-third cup rolled oats
- Amaranth seeds, 1/3 cup
- One teaspoon of salt

Direction

1. For the bread machine, follow the manufacturer's instructions for adding water, molasses, yeast, wheat flour, ground flax seed, bread flour, oat bran, rolled oats, amaranth seeds, and salt. After you choose the Dough cycle and hit Start, the machine should run it through its complete cycle.
2. Before setting the dough on a floured surface, make sure the surface is clean. On a baking stone, lay down two loaves of bread. Allow the loaves to rise for around an hour, covered with a damp cloth, until they have multiplied in size.
3. A temperature of 190°C (375°F) should be used for the oven.
4. To get a golden brown top, pre-heat the oven and bake the bread for 20 to 25 minutes. Gently tap the bread from bottom to top after placing it on a clean surface. Once the loaf sounds hollow when pressed, it's done.

Nutrition Information

- Cal: 101 calories;
- Carbs:18.2 g
- Fat: 2.1 g
- Protein: 4 g

40.High Protein Bread

- Serving: 10
- Prep: 10m
- Ready in: 2h40m

Ingredients

- Two tsp dry active yeast
- 250 g of flour for bread
- 250 g of flour made from whole wheat
- One-fourth cup soy flour
- 1/4 cup of soy milk powder
- One-fourth cup oat bran
- One tablespoon of canola oil
- One tablespoon of honey
- One teaspoon of salt
- 250 g of water

Direction

1. The manufacturer recommends placing ingredients in the bread machine pan in sequence. Set the machine on normal or basic medium. Press Start.

Nutrition Information

- Cal: 137 calories;
- Carbs:24.1 g

- Fat: 2.4 g
- Protein: 6.5 g

41.Cinnamon Raisin Bagels

- Yields 10 bagels

Ingredients

- Two tsp dry yeast
- one and a half tablespoons sugar
- one and a quarter cups warm water
- three and a half cups bread flour
- one and a half tablespoons of salt
- One tsp ground cinnamon and a splash of nutmeg
- one-third cup raisins

Directions

2. Be patient as the yeast, sugar, and warm water bubble in a stand mixer. Before adding the flour, salt, spices, and raisins, wait 5-10 minutes for the mixture to foam. Then, stir on low for 6-8 minutes.
3. Cover the dough with plastic and set it in a basin that has been lightly greased. After an hour, increase it again until it doubles.
4. On a floured surface, pound down the rising dough. Make balls out of 8–10 pieces of dough. Using your finger or thumb, carefully punch a hole in the center to form a bagel. Using a baking tray, shape each bagel. To rise, cover with a tea towel.
5. Turn the oven on to 425F. Cook each bagel in a large saucepan of boiling water for one to two minutes, turning once. grease or parchment for baking pans. Bake for 15 to 20 minutes, or until brown.

Nutritional Information

- Calories 202
- Fat 0.5g
- Protein 5.2g

42.Chocolate Chip Bagels

- Yields 8-10 bagels

Ingredients

- Two tsp of dry active yeast

- 1 1/4 cups warm water, 35 g sugar, and 3 1/2 cups all-purpose (or bread) water flour
- two tsp salt
- one tsp finely ground cinnamon
- 3/4 cup chocolate chips

Directions

1. Warm water, sugar, and yeast should be combined in a stand mixer basin; allow to foam. Add the flour, salt, spices, and raisins; let it bubble for 5 to 10 minutes, then stir on low for 6 to 8 minutes.
2. Spoon dough into a basin that has been lightly oiled, then cover with plastic wrap. Give it an hour or so to rise until it has doubled.
3. Pound the dough that is rising on a surface that has been sprinkled with flour. Gather nine or ten pieces of dough and roll each into a ball. To make the dough into a bagel shape, use your thumb or finger to lightly press a hole in the center. Place every one of the bagels on a baking sheet. Put a tea towel over it to make it stand.
4. Set the oven temperature to 425°F. Cook the bagels in a big pot of boiling water for a minute or two, turning once. Coat baking pans with oil or use parchment paper to line them. Cook in the oven for about 15 to 20 minutes, or until done.

Nutritional Information

- Calories 80
- Fat 3.8g
- Protein 1.3g

43. Hamburger Buns

- Yields 12 buns

Ingredients

- 250 g plus two teaspoons of warm water and two tablespoons of active dry yeast
- one-third cup of vegetable oil
- one-fourth cup sugar
- One egg
- one tsp salt
- 3 to 3-1/2 cups all-purpose flour

Directions

1. The first step is to froth the yeast, sugar, and warm water in a bowl of a stand mixer. Add the other ingredients after it has foamed for five to ten

minutes, and then mix on low for six to eight minutes using the dough hook attachment.

2. While working on a floured surface, divide the dough into ten or twelve equal pieces. Get a baking sheet ready and then wrap and place the ingredients. Tend to yourself for a while by folding the cover.

3. Bake for 8–10 minutes after preheating the oven to 425°F.

Nutritional Information

- Calories 77
- Fat 6.1g
- Protein 1.1g

44. Pretzel Balls

- Yields 24-36 bites

Ingredients

- 1. half a cup heated water
- One tablespoon sugar and two teaspoons salt
- One box of dry active yeast
- 4–4. half a cup of flour
- Ten cups water and two ounces of unsalted butter melted
- two and a third cups baking soda
- One large egg yolk whisked with one tablespoon of water
- Pretzel salt

Directions

1. In a stand mixer, combine the water, sugar, yeast, and kosher salt. Allow the mixture to froth for five minutes.

2. Mix the flour and butter gently using the dough hook attachment until thoroughly combined. To get a smooth dough, knead it for four to five minutes on medium speed, or until it pulls away from bowl edges.

3. Once the dough is taken out of the bowl, coat it with oil. After you've added more flour to the bowl, cover it with plastic and set it aside for an hour. The size of the dough should double.

4. Preheat oven to 450 degrees Fahrenheit. In a large saucepan, bring up to a boil ten cups of water together with the baking soda.

5. On a floured surface, divide the dough into eight equal halves. After being sliced into 1-inch segments, each rope of dough should measure 24 inches in length.

6. Warm the pretzels in batches of 30 seconds each in the boiling water. After removing them from the water using a slotted spoon, place them on a

parchment-lined baking sheet in an arranged fashion that avoids touching one another.

7. After seasoning the pretzel nibbles with salt, drizzle them with the mixture of beaten egg yolk and water. Cook until golden brown, about 6 to 10 minutes.

Nutritional Information

- Calories 77
- Fat 1.7g
- Protein 1.8g

45. Parmesan Flatbread

- Yields 1 flatbread

Ingredients

- Two tsp of dry active yeast
- 1 cup of hot water
- 2 tbsp sugar
- 3 half a cup of white bread flour
- One tablespoon of salt with garlic
- one-fourth cup olive oil
- one-fourth cup parmesan

Directions

1. To prove, combine sugar, yeast, and warm water in a standing mixer fitted with a dough hook.
2. Mix the yeast, sugar, and water in a stand mixer; let aside for 5 minutes, or until frothy. Knead the dough for another 6 to 8 minutes after adding the remaining bread ingredients. Flourish until dough is smooth and slightly tacky. If the batter is too sticky or too dry, adjust the flour to water ratio. After removing the dough from the bowl, cover it with plastic wrap or a tea towel and set it in a lightly greased basin. Wait an hour for it to rise. Expect the dough to double in size.
3. Shape the dough into a 10-inch rectangle or oblong that is 1/2 to 1 inch thick on a floured surface. This will allow you to make flatbread. If you don't have a baking stone, transfer the dough to a baking pan. Rest it on the counter for a while.
4. In the meantime, bring the oven up to 400 degrees and cover with a tea towel to allow it rise for around 15 to 20 minutes.
5. Remove the dough from the oven and use your fingertips to make dimples in it. Before generously topping the dough with the other ingredients, drizzle it with olive oil.
6. Brown the top by baking for 15–25 minutes.

Nutritional Information

- Calories 128
- Fat 3.2g
- Protein 2.9g

46. Ciabatta

- Yields 1 loaf

Ingredients

- One and a half tsp active dry yeast
- One tsp of kosher salt
- 3/4 tsp of sugar, granulated
- 3 1/4 cups all-purpose flour, 1 3/4 cups warm water
- Two tsp olive oil plus additional for the bowl

Directions

1. To start the proofing process, put a dough hook to a standing mixer and combine sugar, yeast, and warm water.
2. Mix the yeast, sugar, and water in a stand mixer; allow to stand for approximately 5 minutes, or until it begins to foam. While the olive oil is being added, knead the dough for a few minutes. The dough needs to become soft and malleable. Transfer the dough to a basin that has been lightly oiled. Poke and press the dough to make holes in it. After the oil has been drizzled, cover with plastic wrap or tea towels. Leave at least half an hour first thing in the morning. The size of the dough should double.
3. Get a baking sheet lined with parchment or silicone paper and get the oven preheated to 400 degrees Fahrenheit.
4. On a floured surface, roll out the dough into a rectangle that is 11 by 4 inches. Before baking, you can coat them with flour if you like. Toast for 35 to 40 minutes, or until browned.

Nutritional Information

- Calories 93
- Fat 0.8g
- Protein 2.6g

47. Cheddar Jalapeno Cornbread

- Yields 12-18 servings

Ingredients

- 250 g of flour for all purposes
- 250 g of cornmeal
- One tsp baking soda and two tbsp of sugar
- One teaspoon of raising agent
- One teaspoon salt and one-fourth teaspoon ground pepper
- Half a cup of buttermilk
- two tsp butter
- 2 large eggs
- 1 1/2 cup grated cheddar cheese
- 2 tbsp minced jalapenos

Directions

1. Grease a 9-by-9-inch baking pan and set oven temperature to 425 degrees.
2. In a large bowl, combine the cornmeal, sugar, baking soda, flour, and rising agent. In a large bowl, combine the cornmeal, sugar, baking soda, flour, egg whites, salt, and pepper.
3. Toss in the eggs, buttermilk, and melted butter, then mix thoroughly. Add the shredded cheese and jalapeños, just stirring gently. Bake for 20 to 25 minutes after batter is added to a pan that has been prepared.

Nutritional Information

- Calories 181
- Fat 8.2g
- Protein 7.5g

48. Quick Whole Wheat Scones

- Yields 8-10 scones

Ingredients

- 250 g of whole wheat flour and two cups of all-purpose flour
- 2 and a half a teaspoon of raising agent
- Half a teaspoon of baking soda
- One tsp salt
- One-half cup cold, diced butter
- 250 g of buttermilk
- One egg and 1/4 cup honey

Directions

1. Combine the flours, baking soda, rising agent, and salt in a large bowl. Add butter and cut until coarse crumbs form. To make a shaggy dough, add the egg, honey, and buttermilk and stir.

2. Cut the dough from a 1/2-inch circular into wedges. Will yield 8–10 uniform pieces. Place on a baking pan coated with paper.
3. Oven: Preheat to 400°F. Bake for 18 to 20 minutes.

Nutritional Information

- Calories 249
- Fat 10.2g
- Protein 5.0g

49.Beginner's Bread

- Yields 1 loaf

Ingredients

- One package of active dry yeast and 3/4 cup of warm water
- 2 teaspoons salt
- 1 tablespoon sugar
- 1 tablespoon butter, softened
- half a cup of milk
- a trio of cups all-purpose flour

Directions

1. Use a stand mixer to combine the yeast, sugar, salt, and water. Wait five minutes for the mixture to froth.
2. After adding 3 cups of flour and butter, beat on low speed with the dough hook attachment until everything is well combined. If more flour is required, add it. The dough should pull away from the edges of the bowl and become smooth after four or five minutes of kneading.
3. Coat the dough with oil after removing it from the bowl. Spread the dough out again in the bowl, then cover with plastic and set aside for one hour. Doubling the dough is the goal.
4. Heat the oven to 450 degrees Fahrenheit.
5. Pound the dough on a board sprinkled with flour. To shape the dough into a loaf, work it once or twice. After putting some oil on the loaf pan, give it 30 minutes to rise. Bake for thirty to forty-five minutes, or until browned.

Nutritional Information

- Calories 94
- Fat 1.1g
- Protein 2.7g

50. Classic Loaf:

Ingredients:

- White bread flour, 500g/1lb, 2oz, plus additional for dusting
- Two teaspoons of brown sugar
- 300g/10½oz starter for sourdough
- Two teaspoons of salt
- Tasteless grease for lubricating

Directions:

1. In a tub, combine flour, sourdough starter, and 250ml/9fl oz of water. Stir in salt and sugar. Knead the dough on a surface for ten minutes, or until the dough turns translucent when stretched, a phenomenon known as the "windowpane effect."
2. After a damp tea towel, place the dough in a gently oiled tub and let it rest for two to three hours. It will take longer and the dough will not rise as much as with yeasted bread.
3. Transfer the dough to a board and knockback. Using the dough, form two sphere-shaped loaves. Load each loaf with flour, seam side up, and set it in a tub lined with a tea towel or a soft cloth that has been properly floured. The bread will cling without the fabric and be unable to turn out. Give it two and a half hours more to prove.
4. Heat the oven to 230°C/210°F on Fan/Gas 8. Put a baking pan with two ice cubes or cold water on it, and steam the bottom of the oven. The loaves should be placed on a warm baking tray or stone. Score the top of the bread two or three times with a small, sharp knife, then bake. Bake for 35 minutes, or until the loaves have a beautiful crust and sound hollow when tapped.

51. Simple Bread:

Ingredients:

- White flour, 375g/13 oz plus additional for dusting
- 250g/9oz sourdough starter, 7.5g salt, and 130–175ml/4-6fl oz of tepid water
- Using olive oil to knead

Directions:

1. The flour, starter, and salt should be mixed together in a big basin. A soft dough will form as you slowly incorporate the water using your hands.
2. The dough should be smooth and elastic after ten to fifteen minutes of kneading on a lightly greased cutting board or other surface.

3. Move to a bowl that has been oiled and seal. Place in a warm place and let rise until twice in size, about 5 hours. Remove the dirt once the dough has been smoothed out. Dust after forming a ball out of flour.
4. For four to eight hours, let the dough rise in a proving basket or circular bannet dusted with flour. Adjust the bottom oven's temperature to 220C/425F / Gas 7 and position a partially filled tray on the rack.
5. Place the rising dough gently onto a baking tray that has been prepared. Reduce the temperature to 200C/400F / Gas 6 after 30 minutes and bake the loaf for 15 to 20 minutes. Rack-lean to disconnect.

52.Classic Sourdough Bread:

Ingredients:

- 1 cup (8 ounces) of starter for sourdough
- Between five and six cups All-Use Flour
- Warm water, 1 1/2 cups (12 ounces)
- One spoonful of salt
- One tablespoon of optional sugar
- Cornmeal to sprinkle on pans

Directions:

1. A big mixing basin should hold the beginning cup. Add three cups of flour and boiling water. Stiffly beat. Put the sponge to work under plastic wrap. While flexible, allow at least 2 hours and up to 8 hours. More time at low temperatures might make food sourer.
2. Remove the plastic wrap when the dough bubbles and spreads. Mix salt, sugar, and 2 cups remaining flour. The dough should be combined and kneaded until smooth and elastic with your hands, a mixer, or a bread machine. Just add enough flour to prevent dough sticking. Cover and let rise in a lightly greased dish for 1–2 hours until doubled.
3. Divide dough halfway through. Form into an oval loaf and put on a baking pan covered with cornmeal.
4. Give it two hours to double in size.
5. Placing a pan of boiling water on the bottom oven rack is a good idea. Preheat the oven to 450 degrees Fahrenheit. Take the cover off, slice, and bake for approximately 20 minutes, or until golden brown. Take out of the oven and place on a cooling rack.
6. Two mini-loaves and nine rolls.Twenties rolls OR Four small loaves

53.4. Ancient Bread:

Ingredients:

- For dusting, use strong bread or pizza flour.

Leaven

- Two tablespoons (50 g) of active sourdough starter
- 80 g (80 ml/⅓ cup) of bread or pizza flour 75 g (100 g) warm water

Dough

- ·700 g (4⅔ cups) bread or pizza flour + extra for dusting
- 2½ tsp. fine sea salt
- 500 g (500 ml/2 cups) warm water

Directions:

1. In a medium dish, stir together the flour, water, and sourdough starter until well blended. Keep the plastic wrap at room temperature for the entire night. Leaven would have formed and bubbled, ready to use.

2. In a big pot, add the leaven to make flour. Break up the leaven with half of the water with a spatula or balloon whisk until it's virtually smooth. Stir in any leftover steam. To form a shaggy dough, add flour and salt to the leaven mixture and stir with a wooden spoon. For one hour, keep the plastic bowl covered in a dry, draft-free area.

3. Spread and fold the dough rather than kneading it. After folding the dough, leave it in the bowl and lift and fold the top side. After each fold, flip the bowl a quarter turn three times. Under plastic wrap, place in a warm, draft-free area for half an hour.

4. Allow the dough to rest for 30 minutes in between each fold. Five more times, repeat. The dough will be shaggy and loose at first, but it will tighten as you fold it and let it to rest. Six folding and resting procedures will produce elastic, smooth, and spongy dough.

5. After folding the dough six times, cover it and set it aside in a warm, draft-free area to rise for one hour.

6. Gently turn out the dough from the bowl onto a flour-dusted board. With a sharp knife or pastry scraper, split the dough in half without letting the pieces swell. Shape each dough piece into a loose circle using your hands (or a pastry scraper) that have been well-floured. Place an oversized bowl (refer to figure 10) on top of every dough ball and let it sit on the bench for a minimum of one to two hours, or until it reaches its maximum puffiness.

7. Dust two clean, loosely woven cloths or tea towels with flour using your fingertips. Two spherical colanders or dough-proving baskets with cloths that are 22 cm high.

8. One dough piece should be floured. Fold the dough again, pressing the sides into the center to crimp the dough surface below, then turn it over to shape it into a circular loaf. Fold just six times to get the maximum air capture. After gently turning the loaf over one more time to level the top, gently stretch the top of the dough in the direction of the bottom to form a level surface and a circle. Proceed with the remaining dough. After lightly dusting the tops and edges of the loaves with flour, place them into the prepared sieve or basket. Over the extra dough on the sides, lightly fold the tea towels.

9. Place each loaf in its colanders or baskets and wrap it in plastic bags. Give it two to three hours in a dry, draft-free place to prove or rise.

10. Preheat the oven to 240°C (220°F with a fan). Line two firm baking pans with parchment paper. Carefully arrange loaves onto prepared trays. Make 1.5 cm deep slashes on loaves with a sharp knife. Place the loaves in the oven, cover with a large quantity of ice cubes, and shut the door. Bake for a further twenty minutes.

11. Replace the pans, reduce the temperature to 220 °C (fan-forced 200 °C), and bake for 15 to 20 minutes, or until the cake is hollow to the touch and has a deep brown color. Before slicing, let the loaves cool on a wire rack.

54. Sourdough Beer Bread Recipe:

Ingredients:

- 12 ounces beer (room temp)
- 1 cup starter for sourdough
- half a cup of sugar
- 5 cups bread flour (approximately)

Directions:

1. Making Bread Dough: This recipe just requires four ingredients, so you'll spend more time kneading than mixing.
2. Use a large tub for the beer and sourdough starter. Remove sugar to dissolve.
3. Mix flour enough to make a hand-kneadable dough.
4. Turn and knead the dough for 10 minutes on a floured surface. Knead the dough until it's no longer sticky, adding flour one tablespoon at a time. Relax as your dough (or "proof" in bread baking) rises. This sourdough with some kneading and shaping needs two proving periods like most bread.
5. Turn the dough over in a bowl to grate the rim.
6. Leave it covered with a kitchen towel or plastic wrap in a dry, draft-free place for 1 1/2 hours to double in size.

7. Roll and knead dough for 5 minutes on floured surface. Slice the dough in half and make a loaf every second. Grease two bread pans and put loaves in pots.
8. Cover with a cloth and let go for 45 minutes to double. Finally bake your dough when it proves. Your kitchen will smell like fresh bread and hops immediately.
9. Bread baking: Oven is preheated at 350 F. Bake the bread for 45 minutes or until hollow when squeezed. Remove the loaves and cool on a rack or cloth. Save the loaves by bagging and freezing.

55.Sourdough Rolls:

Ingredients:

- 450 grams of bread flour
- 250 grams of room-temperature milk
- 150 grams of active starter for sourdough
- 50 grams softened butter
- 10 grams of salt and 35 grams of sugar
- One big egg

Directions:

1. assemble the ingredients; grease a 9 by 13-inch baking pan.
2. Combine all ingredients in a bowl of a stand mixer with a dough handle. Increase the speed to second or third (vigorous but not quick) after two minutes of low speed mixing, and continue mixing for four to five minutes. Perfect dough is light and fluffy. It's ideal to have some stickiness.
3. Scrape the dough into a shallower, larger basin. Put a damp cloth or plastic bag over the saucepan. After dough has rested for 20 minutes, stretch and fold it. Dough is fermented for 4–5 hours at room temperature, then chilled for 12–16 hours.
4. Cut the chilled dough into twelve 80-gram portions. Roll into balls and arrange in a single layer on the pan. Cover and allow to rise in a warm place for two hours (ideally between 80 and 85 degrees Fahrenheit, but any temperature above 65 degrees is OK) or until the dough has doubled in volume.
5. Preheat oven to 425°F. Bake until golden, 20 to 30 minutes. Warm servings are possible. Before processing, let it cool.

56.Sourdough Banana Bread:

Ingredients:

- 140 grams or so of one ripe banana
- 140 grams of cold-discarded sourdough starter and 130 grams of sugar
- thirty grams of olive oil
- 20 grams of melted butter
- Blackstrap molasses, 10 grams
- One big egg
- one-eighth teaspoon pure vanilla
- half a teaspoon of cinnamon powder
- 75 grams of flour for bread
- Half a teaspoon of raising agent
- One-half tsp baking soda
- 60 grams of chopped walnuts and 1/4 teaspoon of salt

Instruction:

1. Heat oven to 350 degrees Fahrenheit. In a big basin, mix the sugar and banana with a fork or whisk until smooth. It is not necessary to purée the banana; some chunks are OK.
2. Mix in starter sourdough, olive oil, butter, molasses, sugar, chocolate, and cinnamon. Whisk together. An electric mixer can be used, although whisking by hand works well.
3. Mix bread flour, salt, and baking soda in a cup. Mix thoroughly.
4. To properly combine the walnuts, add the dry ingredients. Stir again to distribute.
5. Butter and lightly flour an 8-x-4-inch loaf pan. Level and distribute batter on top. Bake loaf center until 200 F, about 45 minutes.
6. Cool before placing on a fridge rack. Let cool fully before serving.

57.Sourdough Bagels:

Ingredients:

- A 110-gram starter for sourdough
- 330 grams of bread flour and 165 grams of water
- 8 grams of sea salt and 25 grams of honey
- One spoonful of baking soda
- Not required: onion, poppy seeds, sesame seeds, etc.

Directions:

1. In a large bowl, combine sourdough starter, milk, honey, water, and salt. Knead dough with your hands for 5 minutes after stirring with a spoon.
2. Cover the saucepan with a wet towel or plastic bag and let it rest for thirty minutes. Dough is stretched and folded. Take another half hour to relax. Six 100-gram portions of dough should be divided.

3. For the bagels, roll each lump into a 12-inch rope. Lightly moisten both rope ends, then draw them together to form a loop. Add more than simply tips. The seam is tightened by overlaying the ends.
4. Put parchment paper on a platter. Spray-oiled paper is delicately greased. Put bagels on paper and wrap them in plastic.
5. Leave them in the fridge overnight after 90 minutes of rising.
6. Oven warms to 500 F.
7. Remove bagels from shelf. Get a huge pot of tea going. Mix in baking soda. Flip the bagels halfway through 2 minutes of poaching. Detach and return to greased sheet tray using wire spider or slotted knife. Sprinkle toppings.
8. Bake 15-18 minutes till golden. Cool on wire rack.

58.Sourdough Loaf

Ingredients:

- 15 oz (425 grammes) of bread flour
- 9 grams/1/3 ounce of salt
- 10 ounces (285 grams) of starter for sourdough
- Olive oil for lubrication

Directions:

1. In a big basin, combine flour and salt. Create a center well, then proceed. Start with flour to create a loose dough. Utilize your hands. Combine the dry ingredients with warm water to form a sticky, smooth dough.
2. Lightly dust your workplace. On a work area, knead dough until it becomes elastic, silky, and smooth. To make sticky dough, add flour. Knead in olive oil if hot. For 12 to 15 minutes, knead.
3. Once the dough is silky, elastic, and smooth, lightly oil a large mixing bowl. Wrap the dough in the tub with plastic or film.
4. To double the dough, place the bowl in a warm, draft-free location for six hours. Overnight in a colder temperature, bread slowly rises.
5. To double, turn dough out onto a floured surface. After taking out the bread crumbs, give the dough a few minutes of gentle kneading. A ball of floured dough should be placed in a bannet or mixing basin. Tea made using cloth. Allow to rise gradually for eight hours in a cool, but not chilly, environment.
6. Preheat the oven to 475°F. Place a roasting dish filled with ice cubes on the lowest oven shelf. Bread gets a wonderful crust from steam.
7. Remove greaseproof paper and lightly oil a baker. Place the rising loaf gently on the sheet (don't worry if it loses air—it'll be baked again). Cook the bread 30 minutes in the hot oven center, then lower the temperature to 400 F and cook for 20 minutes until it sounds hollow when tapered and is golden brown.

8. Cool the loaf on a rack before eating. A week of sourdough is feasible. Avoid plastic since it weakens crust. Place in paper bag or bread bin. The bread keeps fresh and toasts well after a week.

59.Amish Sourdough Bread:

Ingredients:

- (1/4 ounce) packaged yeast
- 2 teaspoons salt and sugar each
- 7 cups flour
- 250 g of room temperature sourdough starter
- 1 1/2 cups water (110 to 115F)
- 1/2 teaspoon baking soda

Directions:

1. Make leaves melt in boiling water.
2. Combine flour, salt, sugar, and sourdough starter in 2 1/2 cups.
3. Mix the sourdough with flour and 2 1/2 cups baking soda. Use a spoon to mix in 1/2–1 cup flour.
4. Knead remaining flour into a compact, smooth, elastic dough (6–8 minutes) on a lightly floured board.
5. Place formed balls in the grated tub. After one turn, cover with plastic wrap or a fresh sheet. Give it one to one and a half hours to double in a warm environment.
6. Take that, half-flour. Take ten minutes to rest under shelter.
7. Grease two circular loaf pans, 9 by 5 inches or 6 by 8 inches. Form the dough. Create a smooth knife with an X-slash. Give it an hour to rise until doubled.
8. Preheat oven to 400 degrees Fahrenheit. Bake loaves for 35–40 minutes. Stylish rack wire.
9. Serve and relish.

60. Landbrot - Wheat Sourdough Bread:

Ingredients:

For Freshening the Sourdough:

- Half a cup of active sourdough culture
- A handful of flour, added and mixed until firm.

For Leaven Build:

- 3-tablespoons/1.3-ounce sourdough mixture
- Four ounces (1/2 cup) of water
- 1 1/3 cups/5.8 ounces whole wheat flour; 2 1/35 g/0.6 ounces white flour

For Final Dough:

- 2 and 3/4 cups (22.4 ounces) of water
- 3 c. + 2 tbsp./14.4 oz. whole wheat flour
- 2.5 c. - 2 tbsp./11 oz. flour (white)
- 3 g./20 g. salt

Directions:

1. Start by Freshening the Sourdough

Collect materials.

2. Maintain hydration for your sourdough starter. When feeding it, add flour and water to make a thick pancake batter. To make the batter steep, start with a half cup of sourdough culture and add flour as needed.
3. Instead of adding flour to a crop right out of the refrigerator, feed it recently. Make the dough stiff.
4. Cover and leave the table for four to six hours.
5. Prepare the leaven:
6. In a bowl, whisk together 1 1/2 cups flour, 1/2 cup water, and 3 tablespoons fresh sourdough (1.3 oz). The dough should be covered and left on the table for 12 hours.
7. Attach 2 3/4 cups water, 3 cups (22.4 ounces + 2 pieces whole wheat flour (14.4 ounces), and 2.5 cups—second T—the next day. Add 11 ounces of white flour to a large mixing bowl and whisk to fully incorporate the flour. Dough should "autolyze" for 20 to 60 minutes under cover.
8. Season with salt and "leaven." Mix by hand for 5 minutes or in a mixer for 2-3 minutes. slack dough.
9. At normal temperature, bulk fermentation takes two and a half hours. The dough needs to be folded twice for this.
10. Flour a board and fold the dough in half. Before dividing and folding the dough vertically, fold it in thirds horizontally (like a letter).
11. The remaining bread dough weighs around 3.5 pounds. Although smaller loaves might be created, we opted to make a large one for the sake of the images.
12. Lastly, proof and shaping:
13. The dough has a loose, spherical texture. Turn the seam side down and set in a floured and oiled measuring cup or a proving tub with plenty of water.
14. To avoid dough touching the bread, loosely cover it. You can use a cardboard box just fine.

15.　　Allow the dough to rise for a minimum of 2.5 to 3 hours in a room temperature setting.

16.　　To get the oven ready to use steam, preheat it to 440 F an hour before baking. Using flour, cornmeal, or semolina, dust the surface. Take out of the proofing basket the dough shape and set it on parchment paper. Be careful not to deflate the dough as it is sticky and wet.

17.　　After covering the baking stone with parchment paper, quickly transfer the baking sheet or dough to the oven. Using steam during baking is recommended in this article.

18.　　After 15 minutes, lower the oven temperature to 420 F and continue baking for another 60 to 75 minutes, or until done. The bread and its inside should reach a temperature of 195 F or higher, as measured using an instant-read thermometer.

19.　　Set the bread out on a rack to cool for at least a few hours. The flavor of bread is enhanced as it ages. Frozen bread is an option.

61. Stuffed Italian Sourdough Loaf:

Ingredients:

- One huge boule of sourdough
- 1/3 cup giardiniera, ¼ pound salami, and ¼ pound prosciutto
- Half a cup of lettuce
- ¼ cup of new basil
- One-half pound of provolone
- One-half pound of mozzarella
- A tablespoon of oil
- One tablespoon of balsamic

Directions:

1. Carve a broad hole in the boule's top and set aside the bread. Hollow out the boule (you may reserve the dough for breadcrumbs).
2. Add the sandwich's remaining ingredients and oil and vinegar.
3. Put the sandwich back on the bread and quarter it.

62. Basic Sourdough Bread:

Ingredients:

- half a cup of milk
- Two tablespoons of shortening
- Add 1 tsp salt and 2 tbsp sugar.

- 1 cup starter for sourdough
- two to three cups bread flour

Directions:

1. Scald and shorten milk in a small pot. Set aside and cool until torrential.
2. Add salt and sugar to a big pot. Pour heated milk and shortening till cold. Sugar dissolves when removed.
3. Stir in starter.
4. Put in half a cup of flour until you can no longer work the dough with a wooden spoon.
5. For 10 minutes, on a floured surface, knead the dough, adding more flour as needed to make it stick.
6. In a bowl, place the dough and oil it. Allow to rise for 90 minutes covered in a warm place. Knead the dough. After 30 minutes, uncover the bowl and let it rise again.
7. Turn board on, knead for 3 minutes.
8. Round loaves of dough are made. Put on baked grated board. Cover and let grow 60 minutes to double. Heat 400F.
9. After 40 minutes in the oven, or when the bread sounds hollow when tapped, make a sharp X in the top.

63. Potato Flake Sourdough Starter and Bread:

Ingredients:

For the Starter:

- 250 g of hot water
- half a cup of sugar One packet of dried yeast (2 1/4 tsp)
- Three tsp of quick potato flakes

For the Starter Feeder:

- 250 g of hot water
- half a cup of sugar
- Three tablespoons of quick potato crisps

For the Bread:

- 250 g of starter (see the notes below).
- bread flour in six cups
- One spoonful of salt and half a cup of sugar
- 1/2 cup oil and 1/4 cup warm water.

Directions:

Note: although this recipe has several steps, this bread is broken down into workable categories to help you organize your cooking and preparation better.

1. Gather Starter ingredients.
2. Mix warm water, sugar, yeast, and potato flakes in a small cup. Wait two days to ferment on the counter.
3. Begin with feeder (down). Skip this move if someone else starts. Gather Starter Feeder ingredients.
4. Mix warm feeder water, sugar, and potato flakes in a small cup. Connect to the starter and mix. Leave it on the counter for 8 hours. Refrigerate 3–5 days, then dark.
5. After using 1 cup of beginning for bread (see below), discard and chill everything except 1 cup of the residual starter.
6. Add the beginning feeding mixture every 3–5 days to create additional bread. Refrigerate after leaving well overnight or 12 hours at the counter.
7. Bread: Combine 1 cup starter, salt, sugar, oil, and warm water in a large basin or mixer. Blend well. Knead by hand or dough hook for 5–10 minutes until smooth and elastic.
8. Grease a bowl and add dough. Cover and let it develop overnight or 12 hours in a warm area.
9. Hit it with a punch. Knead to get rid of air bubbles on a floured surface.
10. Evenly divide the dough among three cooking spray-coated loaf pans. For six to eight hours, let the loosely sealed rise.
11. Bake for 25 to 30 minutes at 350 F. Take out of the oven and pan and let cool on a wire rack.

64. Extra-Tangy Sourdough Bread:

Ingredients:

- 250 g (227g) of fed, ripe sourdough starter
- 5 cups (602g) of warm water, or 1 1/2 cups (340g). 2 1/2 teaspoons of salt and all-purpose flour divided

Directions:

1. Combine the flour, water, and three tassels (12 3/4 oz, 362 g). For one minute, beat vigorously. Cover for four hours at room temperature. Allow to chill over night for 12 hours.
2. Combine the remaining 2 cups (8 1/2 ounces, 241 g) flour with the salt. Work into a silky dough. In a covered bowl, let the dough rise until it becomes light and bubbly with gas. This may take up to five hours or more, depending on

the vigor of your starter. To achieve optimal outcomes, gently deflate the dough once per hour by transferring it to a lightly floured surface, stretching and folding the sides inward, and then turning it over before putting it back in the pot. Seeing the dough's development is made easier by adding folds.

65.San Francisco style sourdough bread:

Ingredients:

- yields one loaf with 65.2% hydration.
- Starter (weight in total: 233 g)
- 264 grams of bread flour
- 50 grams of spelt flour (whole grain preferred)
- 204 grams of water
- nine grams of salt

Directions:

Making the Loaf:

1. So, on day three of the recipe, it's probably afternoon (17.00 h if you follow my timetable). Once the starter is taken out of the refrigerator, launch the dough right away. Mix 204 g water with the starting and play for one minute to release the stiff starter. Use a spiral blender to mix the flour and salt for three minutes. For fifteen minutes, leave the mixer bowl covered.

2. Fold the dough in the following directions: top over bottom, bottom over top, left over right, and full letter fold. Cover and leave on the bench for fifteen minutes. Fold after the second stretch. After covering the oiled pot, leave it for forty minutes at room temperature. To let the bacteria to continue producing acetic acid, which gives your bread its sour flavor, and to allow the yeast cells to hibernate, place the dough in the refrigerator for 15 hours (yes, you can sleep during this time). SF Sourdough Ma's fourth day. Use your finger to make a little tooth-shaped indent in the dough if it has risen sufficiently. If there is still a tooth in the bread, it is ready to bake; if not, it needs to bake for longer.

3. Preheat your oven to 235C/455F (many take 30 minutes, while others with stone flooring need two hours). Three hours are needed to prepare the bread for baking. Your loaf is oven-ready. When using a baking tray to produce steam, you may need to raise the oven temperature to compensate for heat loss.

4. Prepare your bread for 45 minutes of baking. Let it cool on the rack. The freezer keeps this bread nicely confined. Please eat some of it while it's fresh!

66.Sourdough Flatbread:

Ingredients:

- 120 grams of warm water and 180 grams of bread flour
- 15 grams of extra virgin olive oil
- 60 grams of sourdough starter.
- Five milligrams of sea salt

Directions:

1. Put the ingredients in a medium dish (a glass bowl is best to see fermentation bubbles). Thoroughly combine. Rugged, puffy, sticky dough.
2. Rest bowl 20 minutes in towel or plastic bag.
3. Next, stretch and fold the dough. Scoop your sweaty hand beneath the dough and carefully grip one side of the lump. Fold the dough over after extending it away from the main mass. Repeat on different dough sides three or four times.
4. Then place the dough bulk fold-side down against the bowl's rim. Shaggy dough is smoother, which is the goal. If dough seems shaggy, try again with a visual assistance.
5. Rest 20 more minutes, stretch, and fold.
6. Cover again and cure at room temp 3-4 hours. Your dough won't rise much, but bubbles appear on and below the top (if in a glass dish). Boil till bubbles appear.
7. A task surface blooms softly. Flip the bowl over the floured surface and wait for it to release. Divide dough twice. Shape pieces into rounds using the same stretch and fold method (without moist hands).
8. Oil two round, one-pint storage containers (ideally lids) and place a seam-side dough ball in each. Wrap in plastic.
9. Refrigerate 24 hours before use. Dough refrigerated for a week or longer develops flavor.
10. Remove pizza dough from the fridge and place on a floured board. Also dust the dough lightly. Please flatten and stretch the dough into a 12-inch round.
11. Add sauce, garnishes, and bake as desired. Immediately serve.

67.Sourdough flatbread pizza

Ingredients:

- 250 g of flour, used for everything
- 1/2 + 1 tablespoon cup Water
- 1/4 cup starter for sourdough

- A half teaspoon of onion powder
- Half a teaspoon of garlic powder
- Just under half a teaspoon of salt
- Two tablespoon of extra virgin olive oil
- Diced tomatoes from a 14.5-ounce can
- 2.5 g. oregano
- 2.5 g. sugar
- 2 tbsps. chopped fresh basil
- 1 pinch salt
- 3 gs. tomato paste
- 2.5 tbsps. balsamic vinegar
- 4 oz. ball of fresh mozzarella slice
- Any topping

Directions:

1. In a dough hook-attached bowl, combine flour, starter, salt, onion and garlic powder, and water on low for 8 minutes. Leave covered at 100 degrees for 15 minutes or bake.
2. To make sauce, heat 35 g oil in a small pot. After heating, boil tomatoes and add 2 tbsp. balsamic vinegar. Reserve remaining. Add remaining sauce ingredients and cook for 10-15 minutes on low.
3. Preheat oven to 550 with cookie sheet inside. Sprinkle flour on big parchment paper.
4. Apply oil to your hands and stretch the dough into a rectangle on paper until you can't. Keep moving the flour outward to make it easier.
5. Add optional sauce, cheese, and topping to bread when ready. Slide flatbread onto cookie sheet with parchment, bake for 5 minutes, remove paper, and bake for 10-15 minutes. Melt 1 cup butter, add 1 cup parmesan, sprinkle of salt, and 1 cup parsley. Brush flatbread crust.
6. Break two eggs immediately into 1/4 cup of heated non-stick oil in a pan and cook for 2-3 minutes. Add cheese, arugula, and balsamic vinegar and drizzle. Cut and enjoy.
7. The sauce suits 2 folding broth. Makes 1.5 tassels. We use strong dry yeast. As thin as possible.

68. Easy Sourdough Flatbread:

Ingredients:

- 2 cups sourdough starter
- one tsp powdered garlic
- One teaspoon Italian seasoning and half a teaspoon salt

- Two tbsp olive oil
- two minced garlic cloves
- 1/4 cup fresh herbs, like rosemary, sage, basil or oregano

Directions:

1. Preheat a cast-iron skillet or 400-degree pizza block.
2. Place thin flatbread shapes of starting ingredients on the prepared block. Add a teaspoon olive oil.
3. Add chopped garlic. Bake until done, about 10 minutes at 400 degrees. Add the chopped herbs and leftover olive oil. Add salt to compare.
4. Slice them and put them in a party basket or eat them plain!

69.Sourdough Flatbread Pizzas:

- Makes 2 to 4 small flatbreads

Ingredients:

- 1/2 cup recently hydrated sourdough starter (here's how)
- One teaspoon of salt
- 1 cup water and 2 100 gs flour

Directions:

1. Mix water, sea salt, and starter sourdough. Add 2 1/2 cups of flour on top. After 5-8 minutes of kneading the dough, add flour as needed. The amount of flour required is determined by the hydration of the sourdough starter, which is fed at different ratios of flour to water.
2. Give the dough a 6-to 8-hour or overnight rest. Preheat oven to 450°F when ready.
3. Separate dough into four balls.
4. Roll out the dough on a surface dusted with flour. Make use of a pizza plate or cookie sheet.
5. Bake for six minutes on the crust. Take the crust out of the oven. Bake with the toppings until the cheese melts and the crust browned. Six to eight minutes, roughly.

70.Starter Sourdough Pizza Crust/Grill bread/Skillet Flatbread:

Ingredients:

- 250 g of sourdough starter—unfed or ignored is ideal in this case—
- One tsp sugar

- 250 g of hot water
- 1.25 cups unbleached all-purpose flour (for the initial ferment)
- 0.75 cups mix of whole-grain flours: buckwheat, spelled or "mixed-grain" are excellent choices, whole wheat flour is just fine too (for the first ferment)
- 1 cup all-purpose flour (for final dough)
- 1 tablespoon salt
- 1 cup high gluten or bread flour (for final dough)
- 1 tablespoon olive oil
- Toppings, extra olive oil for brushing on grilled dough

Directions:

1. Stir starter and 1.25 cup all-purpose flour in a large bowl.75 cup grain flour and warm water till homogeneous. Cover with a moist towel for 2 hours. If you're confident in your beginning, it should work out well if you don't notice bigger bubbles as they start. Try waiting long before the beginning wakes up.

2. After stirring the starter, add the remaining flour, salt, sugar, and olive oil. You may stir dry herbs or seeds here. It may need extra flour to form a dough ball that's too hard to combine.

3. Knead for 6 minutes on a floured surface until stiff and consistent. Avoid adding too much flour, however you may need to add enough to prevent sticking depending on humidity, starter, etc. Rather than sticky, tacky is best.

4. Refrigerate overnight in a large bag, assuming slight expansion.

5. Remove from refrigerator 30 minutes before baking/cooking. It will be mild and loose, but OK! Let it reach room temperature (even a touch chilly is fine—it will warm up when you work with it).

6. Cover and divide into 5-6 pieces until needed. Unneeded pieces can be frozen at this level. Smaller pieces are simpler to work with after becoming acquainted to the dough.

7. Pizza is baked in a 475-500 degree oven on a prepared cook surface (pizza stone, sturdy upside-down cookie sheet). Due to its low rise, this dough needs to cook longer. Stretch and pull the dough into a thin circle on a floured board. Use a well-dusted pizza peel or cornmeal or semolina peel. After a short olive oil brushing and toppings (go easy on the watery ones), bake the pizza. Bake for 15 minutes until dough is done and topped.

8. For skillet flatbreads, cut dough into 3 pieces. Use a non-smoking cast-iron skillet over medium heat. Roll each piece (don't work ahead or the dough spreads out) to 1/8-1/16 inch thick on a floured board, flipping the dough a few times. Rolling might include dry spices, herbs, seeds, etc. Flip the dough on the heated skillet for 2–3 minutes to brown. Refrigerate unfilled bread and cook on a dry skillet.

9. Grilled pizza: prepare all toppings close to the grill. You can keep a hand over the grate for 3-4 seconds on a medium-hot grill. Check grills for cleanliness.

Use your hands to gently pull or stretch the dough into a thin crust over the medium-hot grill after dipping it in olive oil. Not wanting to press dough for a few minutes. Cook on edge, caramelize, then release.

10. Brush olive oil on top. Flip and quickly top the pizza with your available sauce, cheese, and whatever you don't require by cooking (it won't get on the grill). Cook for 5 minutes with the grill closed (until you smell burning). Reheat the pizzas in the grill after doing this one at a time. If you BBQ, it may be hot, therefore you don't need hot pizza!

71.Flax Bread

- Time spent preparing: ten minutes
- 45 minutes for cooking
- One bread dish is served.

Ingredients:

- 1 cup flaxseed meal
- 4 eggs, whisked
- 1 cup coconut flour
- One teaspoon of raising agent
- One tsp baking soda
- One tsp salt
- A tsp apple cider vinegar and a quarter cup warm water

Directions:

1. Stir coconut flour, flaxseed meal, and other ingredients except eggs and water in a bowl.
2. Stir in the eggs and water and knead into dough.
3. Bake it for 40 minutes at 350 degrees F in a loaf pan before cooling and serving.

Nutrition/ loaf:

- calories 300,
- fat 12, fiber 1.2,
- carbs 4.3,
- protein 9.2

72.Flax Stevia Bread

- Time spent preparing: ten minutes
- 20 minutes for cooking
- One loaf is served.

Ingredients:

- 1 tablespoon raising agent
- 1 and 100 g protein isolate
- ½ teaspoon salt
- 2 cups flax seed meal
- 4 egg whites, whisked
- 1 whole egg, whisked
- 1 cup water
- ¼ cup stevia
- 35 g coconut oil, melted

Directions:

1. Stir flax seed meal, protein isolate, and other dry ingredients in a dish.
2. Stir in the remaining wet ingredients and knead the dough.
3. Bake 20 minutes at 370 degrees F in a large loaf pan.
4. Slice and serve after cooling.

Nutrition/ slice:

- calories 87
- fat 1.2
- carbs 3
- protein 2.2

73.Wheat and Almond Focaccia

- Time spent preparing: two hours
- 40 minutes of cooking
- A pair of focaccia

Ingredients:

- a single cup of wheat flour
- 250 g of almond flour
- Half a teaspoon of salt
- ½ teaspoon cayenne pepper
- Half a cup of olive oil
- two minced cloves of garlic
- One tablespoon of raising agent
- 5 eggs, whisked
- 1 tablespoon rosemary, dried
- Cooking spray

Directions:

1. Stir wheat flour, almond flour, and other ingredients except oil in a bowl.
2. Pour in the oil slowly and mix again.
3. Fill two square pans with this mixture, bake at 330 degrees for forty minutes, let cool, and then serve.

Nutrition/ focaccia:

- calories 243
- fat 5.4
- carbs 5.4
- protein 3.2

74.Corn Shortbread

- Time spent preparing: 30 minutes
- 15 minutes for cooking
- 8 servings

Ingredients:

- 2 cups corn flour
- 5 tablespoons ghee, melt
- One tablespoon of grated lemon zest
- Four tsp sugar
- One tablespoon of lemon juice
- One tsp vanilla essence
- One teaspoon of raising agent
- One tsp dried rosemary

Directions:

1. Step into a bowl and mix together the flour, sugar, rising agent, lemon zest, and rosemary.
2. Make a log shape with the dough and add the other ingredients little by little. Wrap in plastic and put in the freezer for 30 minutes.
3. After slicing the log into rounds, set them on a baking sheet coated with parchment and bake them for 15 minutes at 370 degrees. Allow it to cool before serving.

Nutrition/ piece:

- calories 100
- fat 2.3
- carbs 3.4
- protein 4.3

75. Rye Pumpkin Bread

- Time spent preparing: ten minutes
- 1 hour and 20 minutes for cooking
- Two loaves are served.

Ingredients:

- 1 and 100 gs rye flour
- 100 g pumpkin puree
- 2 eggs, whisked
- 3 tablespoons sugar
- 100 g almond milk, warm
- 100 g psyllium husk powder
- One tsp pumpkin pie spice
- One tsp baking soda
- Half a teaspoon of salt

Directions:

1. Take a bowl and mix together the flour, sugar, baking soda, spices, husk powder, and salt.
2. After transferring to two loaf pans, whisk in the other ingredients until well combined. Bake at 330 degrees Fahrenheit for 45 minutes.
3. Slice and serve once cooled.

Nutrition/ loaf:

- calories 212
- fat 5.4
- carbs 8.54
- protein 4

76. Butter Whole Wheat Buns

- Time spent preparing: ten minutes
- Twelve minutes of cooking
- Four buns are served.

Ingredients:

- 35 g whole wheat flour
- ½ teaspoon baking soda and two tablespoons of melted butter
- Twice as much psyllium husk
- ¼ cup chicken stock

Directions:

4. In a bowl, mix together the flour, melted butter, and additional ingredients; do not stir until well blended.
5. Separate the mixture into four equal balls, flatten them, place them on a greased baking sheet, and bake at 340 degrees for 12 minutes.

Nutrition/bun:

- calories 142
- fat 4.3
- carbs 6.5
- protein 2.3

77.Mozzarella Rye Bagels

- Time spent preparing: ten minutes
- 20 minutes for cooking
- 4 servings

Ingredients:

- 1 cup rye flour
- 1 cup mozzarella, shredded
- 1 tablespoon cream cheese
- One tsp salt
- 1 egg, whisked
- 1 tablespoon sesame seeds
- One teaspoon sugar and one tablespoon melted butter

Directions:

1. Stir flour, mozzarella, and other ingredients except sesame seeds and butter in a bowl until a firm dough forms.
2. Divide 4 parts into donut pans.
3. Butter them, add sesame seeds, and bake at 380 degrees F for 20 minutes.

Nutrition/ bagel:

- calories 200
- fat 4.3
- carbs 5.4
- protein 7.6

78.Chili Quinoa Loaf

- Time spent preparing: ten minutes
- 25 minutes for cooking
- One loaf is served.

Ingredients:

- 1 and 100 gs quinoa, cooked
- 100 g flaxseed meal
- 2 eggs, whisked
- One teaspoon of raising agent
- One tsp baking soda
- 100 g sour cream and one teaspoon salt
- three tablespoons softened butter
- One spoonful of sugar
- 2 red chili peppers, minced
- 100 g cheddar cheese, grated
- Cooking spray

Directions:

1. In a bowl, combine quinoa, baking soda, flax seed meal, rising agent, and other ingredients; mix until a dough forms.
2. In a loaf pan that has been greased, knead the dough for ten minutes. Bake for twenty-five minutes at 375 degrees Fahrenheit.
3. Once cooled, slice and serve.

Nutrition/ loaf:

- calories 200
- fat 12.2
- carbs 8.5
- protein 5.3

79.Soft Rice Bread

- Time spent preparing: ten minutes
- One hour and ten minutes of cooking
- Two loaves are served.

Ingredients:

- 1 100 gs of rice flour
- One tsp salt
- One tsp of vinegar made from apple cider
- One tsp baking soda
- One teaspoon of raising agent
- Three teaspoons powdered psyllium husk
- 1 cup warm water
- 2 eggs, whisked
- 1 egg yolk, whisked

- Cooking spray

Directions:

1. Dissolve the rice husk powder, salt, soda, and rising agent in the rice flour in a big basin.
2. To produce a dough, add the eggs and the other ingredients—aside from the cooking spray—and stir.
3. Work the dough for ten minutes, then transfer it to two oiled loaf pans and bake for one hour and twenty minutes at 350 degrees Fahrenheit.
4. Slice, let cool, and serve the bread.

Nutrition/ loaf:

- calories 172
- fat 4.4
- carbs 5.5
- protein 2.3

80. Coconut Corn Bread

- Time spent preparing: ten minutes
- 50 minutes of cooking
- One loaf is served.

Ingredients:

- 100 g coconut flour
- 100 g corn flour
- One teaspoon of dried oregano
- One tsp dried basil
- 5 eggs, whisked
- Six tablespoons of melted butter
- One tsp baking soda
- one tsp powdered garlic
- One-half teaspoon of black pepper
- Half a teaspoon of salt

Directions:

1. Using a big basin, combine the flour with the other seasonings, oregano, and basil. Knead the dough for 10 minutes after mixing, and then place it in a loaf pan lined with parchment paper.
2. After 50 minutes in the oven at 340 degrees, take it out and let it cool completely before cutting it.

Nutrition/ loaf:

- calories 172
- fat 4.3
- fiber 2.3
- carbs 4.4
- protein 6

81. Dutch Oven Spelt Bread

- Time spent preparing: 30 minutes
- 40 minutes of cooking
- One loaf is served.

Ingredients:

- 125 milligrams of almond flour
- 1 and a half cups spelt flour
- A single tsp of raising agent
- One teaspoon of baking soda
- Half a teaspoon of salt
- 1 teaspoon sugar
- 1 and 100 gs warm water

Directions:

3. Flour, baking soda, and raising agent should be combined in a basin. Handle the mixture with care as you work it into a dough.
4. For an additional half an hour, cover the bowl and allow the dough to rise.
5. After putting everything into a Dutch oven and baking it at 400 degrees for 40 minutes, let it cool down and then cut and serve.

Nutrition/ loaf:

- calories 242
- fat 6.5
- fiber 3.3
- carbs 6.4
- protein 4.3

82. Avocado Whole Wheat Bread

- Time spent preparing: ten minutes
- 40 minutes of cooking
- One loaf is served.

Ingredients:

- 250 g of flour made from whole wheat

- One teaspoon of raising agent
- One tsp powdered cinnamon
- 100 g sugar
- 1 egg, whisked
- ½ teaspoon of vanilla extract and four tablespoons of melted butter
- one tsp lemon juice
- 1 cup avocado, peeled, pitted and mashed

Directions:

1. Combine the flour, cinnamon, rising agent, and other ingredients in a bowl; whisk until a dough forms.
2. After kneading the dough for ten minutes, place it in a loaf pan and bake it for forty minutes at 320 degrees Fahrenheit.
3. Slice, cool, and serve the bread.

Nutrition/ loaf:

- 254 calories and 254 fat 6.5 fiber Protein: 6.5 Carbs: 3.4 Six

83.Parmesan Rice Bread

- Time spent preparing: one hour and ten minutes
- 40 minutes of cooking
- Two loaves are served.

Ingredients:

- 1 cup parmesan, grated
- 1 cup rice flour
- 1 and 100 gs warm water
- One tsp of instant yeast
- One teaspoon of raising agent
- One tsp salt and one tsp black pepper
- one minced clove of garlic

Directions:

1. Combine all of the ingredients, including the water and flour, in a large basin. After mixing until a dough forms, cover the basin and let it sit for one hour.
2. After 50 minutes in the oven at 390 degrees, split the dough in half and bake in separate loaf pans. Let cool completely before cutting and serving.

Nutrition/ loaf:

- calories 272
- fat 5.4
- fiber 2.4

- carbs 5.4
- protein 3.4

84. Whole Wheat Cauliflower Bread

- Time spent preparing: ten minutes
- One hour is needed for cooking.
- One loaf is served.

Ingredients:

- 5 tablespoons olive oil
- 5 eggs, whisked
- 250 g of flour made from whole wheat
- 2 cups cauliflower, grated
- ½ teaspoon salt
- 1 tablespoon baking soda
- One-half teaspoon of black pepper

Directions:

3. Gather all the ingredients, including the cauliflower, and mix in the whole wheat flour. After 10 minutes of mixing and kneading, you should have an elastic dough.
4. After mixing the ingredients, transfer the dough to a loaf pan and bake at 350 degrees Fahrenheit for an hour.
5. Cut and serve after cooling.

Nutrition/ loaf:

- calories 287
- fat 6.5
- fiber 2.3
- carbs 3.4
- protein 5.4

85. Broccoli Rye Bread

- Time spent preparing: ten minutes
- 40 minutes of cooking
- One loaf is served.

Ingredients:

- 1 cup broccoli, grated
- 1 cup cheddar cheese, shredded
- 100 g rye flour

- 5 eggs, whisked
- One tablespoon warm water and two tablespoons baking soda
- Cooking spray

Directions:

1. In a bowl, mix together the broccoli, cheese, and remaining ingredients (except from the cooking spray). Swirl it around a bit and work it into a dough.
2. Grease a loaf pan with cooking spray, put the bread inside, and bake at 350 degrees for 40 minutes.
3. Once the bread has cooled, slice and serve.

Nutrition/ loaf:

- calories 273
- fat 7.6
- fiber 3.4
- carbs 4.4
- protein 5.4

86.Spinach Corn Bread

- Time spent preparing: ten minutes
- 40 minutes of cooking
- Two loaves are served.

Ingredients:

- One tablespoon of olive oil
- One tsp salt
- 100 g finely diced spinach
- 3 cups corn flour
- 250 g of hot water
- One tsp baking soda
- One spoonful of sugar
- 100 g of shredded cheddar

Directions:

1. In a bowl, whisk together the flour, sugar, baking soda, and the remaining ingredients until a soft dough forms.
2. Before serving, let the bread to cool in the pans before slicing it. Preheat the oven to 390 degrees Fahrenheit and bake for 40 minutes.

Nutrition/ loaf:

- calories 300

- fat 6.7
- fiber 3.4
- carbs 5.4
- protein 4.9

87.Nutmeg Asparagus Bread

- Time spent preparing: ten minutes
- 45 minutes for cooking
- One loaf is served.

Ingredients:

- 1 cup sugar
- 1 cup avocado oil
- 2 cups corn flour
- 2 egg whites, whisked
- 1 teaspoon raising agent
- 1 teaspoon nutmeg, ground
- ½ teaspoon salt
- Cooking spray
- 2 cups asparagus, steamed and chopped

Directions:

1. Combine all of the ingredients (apart from the cooking spray) in a large bowl, including the flour, sugar, and oil. Once a dough has formed, cover the bowl and set aside for 10 minutes to rest.
2. Coat a loaf pan with cooking spray and transfer the dough inside. Cook it for 45 minutes at 350 degrees.
3. The bread should be sliced and served after it has cooled.

Nutrition/ loaf:

- calories 200
- fat 3.4
- fiber 3.3
- carbs 8.7
- protein 3.4

88.Eggplant Rye Bread

- Time spent preparing: ten minutes
- One hour is needed for cooking.
- One loaf is served.

Ingredients:

- 35 g sugar
- 100 g warm milk
- 2 eggs, whisked
- 1 and 100 gs rye flour
- 1 teaspoon salt
- 2 eggplants, washed and grated
- 1 teaspoon turmeric powder
- 2 teaspoons raising agent

Directions:

1. In a bowl, whisk together the milk, flour, and the rest of the ingredients. Transfer the batter to a loaf pan.
2. Before serving, bake at 350 degrees Fahrenheit for one hour. Once baked, remove from oven and allow to cool.

Nutrition/ loaf:

- calories 200
- fat 4.4
- fiber 3.3
- carbs 7.5
- protein 4.3

89.Onion Corn Bread

- Time spent preparing: 1 hour
- 40 minutes of cooking
- One loaf is served.

Ingredients:

- Two tablespoons of olive oil and six chopped spring onions
- 1 yellow onion, chopped
- 4 cups corn flour
- Half a teaspoon of salt
- A half-tsp of pepper, white
- 1 and half-cup of warm water
- two tsp of dry yeast

Directions:

1. Combine the spring onions, oil, flour, and remaining ingredients in a bowl. Give it a good toss, knead until a dough forms, cover the bowls, and let them aside for an hour.

2. Place the bread in a loaf pan, bake it for 40 minutes at 375 degrees Fahrenheit, allow it to cool, then cut and serve.

Nutrition/ loaf:

- calories 253
- fat 4.4
- fiber 2.3
- carbs 7.4
- protein 4.3

90. Bean Whole Wheat Bread

- Time spent preparing: ten minutes
- 30 minutes for cooking
- Two loaves are served.

Ingredients:

- One teaspoon baking soda and two cups corn flour
- 1 teaspoon salt
- 2 cups canned Cherokee beans, drained, rinsed and mashed
- ½ teaspoon hot paprika
- 2 eggs, whisked
- Two tbsp olive oil
- 1 and 100 gs milk

Directions:

1. Combine the flour, baking soda, salt, beans, and additional ingredients in a bowl. Stir and knead the mixture until a dough forms.
2. Split between two loaf pans, bake for thirty minutes at 400 degrees Fahrenheit, allow to cool, then cut and serve.

Nutrition/ loaf:

- calories 300
- fat 6.5
- fiber 6.9
- carbs 12.2
- protein 4.5

91. White Country Bread

- Time spent preparing: ten minutes
- Two hours are needed for cooking.
- One loaf is served.

Ingredients:

- 2 and 100 gs white flour
- 1 and 100 gs water
- 1 cup bread flour
- 1 teaspoon raising agent
- Two and a half tsp baking powder
- two tsp sugar
- One tablespoon of olive oil
- One tsp salt

Directions:

1. In the bread machine, mix the flour with bread flour, water and the other ingredients, set the machine on quick setting and medium crust.
2. Push the start button and cool the bread down before serving.

Nutrition/ slice:

- calories 122
- fat 5
- fiber 3.4
- carbs 17
- protein 2

92. Whole Bread

- Time spent preparing: ten minutes
- Two hours are needed for cooking.
- One loaf is served.

Ingredients:

- One and half-cup of warm water
- Two tsp of avocado oil
- 1/3 cup brown sugar and 1 teaspoon salt
- three tsp of coconut milk
- two tsp of dry yeast
- 4 and 100 gs whole wheat flour

Directions:

1. Combine the water, oil, and other ingredients in the bread machine.
2. Before serving, let the bread cool after cooking it in the Whole Wheat mode.

Nutrition/ slice:

- calories 200
- fat 4.3

- carbs 16
- protein 3.4

93.Cereal Bread

- Time spent preparing: ten minutes
- 40 minutes of cooking
- One loaf is served.

Ingredients:

- 125 milliliters of bread flour
- a half-cup of warm water
- two tsp butter
- A cup and a half of whole wheat flour
- 250 g of cereal with many grains
- One tsp salt
- Two teaspoons of bread machine yeast and three tsp sugar

Directions:

1. Combine the flour, water, and other ingredients in your bread machine.
2. Select Basil Cycle and medium crust and start the machine.
3. Cool down and serve.

Nutrition/slice:

- calories 143
- fat 4
- fiber 4.4
- carbs 25
- protein 6

94.Milk Bread

- Time spent preparing: ten minutes
- Two hours are needed for cooking.
- One loaf is served.

Ingredients:

- 250 g coconut milk
- Two tbsp coconut cream
- 3 tablespoons honey
- three tablespoons softened butter
- three cups of bread flour
- One tsp salt

- two tsp dry machine yeast

Directions:

4. Combine the coconut milk, cream, and remaining ingredients in the bread machine. Select the medium crust and white bread settings, then turn the machine on.
5. Once cooled, serve..

Nutrition/ slice:

- calories 70
- fat 3
- fiber 2.3
- carbs 7
- protein 2

95.Potato Rolls

- Time spent preparing: 55 minutes
- 20 minutes for cooking
- Servings: Twenty-four

Ingredients:

- Two cooked, peeled, and mashed sweet potatoes
- 250 g of milk
- three tablespoons softened butter
- Four cups of white flour
- One whisked egg
- One tsp salt
- two tsp of dry yeast

Directions:

1. Use the basil dough cycle in the bread machine after adding the sweet potatoes, milk, and other ingredients.
2. After this cycle, break off pieces of dough, roll them into medium-sized balls, and place them on a baking sheet that has been lined.
3. After letting the dough rise for forty-five minutes, bake it for twenty minutes at 375 degrees Fahrenheit.

Nutrition/roll:

- calories 141
- fat 6
- fiber 3
- carbs 17

- protein 4

96.Pretzels

- Twenty minutes for preparation
- Ten minutes for cooking
- 12 servings

Ingredients:

- One spoonful of sugar
- three cups of white flour
- two tsp of dry yeast
- 1/2 cup water plus 2 quarts
- One tsp salt
- one-third cup of baking soda

Directions:

1. Add the yeast, sugar, flour, 100 g water, and salt to your bread machine. Press the dough cycle button.
2. The cycle is complete when you remove the dough from the machine. Knead it on a floured surface for a few minutes. Divide the dough into 12 equal sections and roll each one into a rope.
3. Before transferring to preheated baking sheets, bring the pretzels, remaining water, and baking soda to a boil in a skillet over medium heat. Simmer, covered, for two minutes.
4. Bake for ten minutes at 475 degrees Fahrenheit.

Nutrition/ pretzel:

- calories 40
- fat 2
- carbs 6
- protein 1

97.Pizza Dough

- Time spent preparing: ten minutes
- 15 minutes for cooking
- Two pizzas are served.

Ingredients:

- Two tsp olive oil
- four cups of flour for bread
- One and a half cups water,

94

- one tablespoon each of sugar and salt, and two teaspoons of active yeast

Directions:

1. After adding all the ingredients, choose the dough cycle on the bread maker.
2. After the cycle is complete, split the dough between two pizza pans.
3. Use the crusts after 15 minutes of baking at 400 degrees Fahrenheit.

Nutrition/ pizza crust:

- calories 40
- fat 2
- fiber 2
- carbs 5
- protein 1

98. Butter Bread

- Time spent preparing: ten minutes
- 40 minutes of cooking
- One loaf is served.

Ingredients:

- 100 g butter, soft
- 3 cups white flour
- 1 teaspoon salt
- 250 g of water
- Two tbsp of brown sugar
- two tsp of active yeast

Directions:

1. In your bread machine, combine all the ingredients, select the Basic bread cycle and light crust and turn the machine on.
2. When the cycle is done, cool the bread down and serve.

Nutrition/ slice:

- calories 152, fat 4, fiber 2, carbs 15, protein 4

99. Milk Onion Savory Bread

- Twenty minutes for preparation
- Two hours are needed for cooking.
- One loaf is served.

Ingredients:

- 35 g coconut oil, melted
- two tsp salt
- 1 and 100 gs water
- One spoonful of sugar
- Four cups of white flour
- two tbsp of dried milk
- two tsp of active yeast
- 4 tablespoons dry onion soup mix

Directions:

1. Put all the ingredients into your bread machine, choose the Medium crust and Bread cycle, and turn it on.
2. Cool the bread down before serving.

Nutrition/ slice:

- calories 152, fat 4, fiber 3, carbs 15, protein 7

100.   Parmesan Bread

- Time spent preparing: ten minutes
- 3 hours for cooking
- One loaf is served.

Ingredients:

- Two tablespoons of avocado oil
- Three minced garlic cloves, one and a half cups water, heated
- Three teaspoons of chopped chives
- One tablespoon of finely chopped basil
- One tablespoon brown sugar and one teaspoon salt
- Two tsp of dry active yeast
- Four cups of white flour
- four tsp grated parmesan

Directions:

1. Combine all the ingredients in your bread machine, choose the medium crust and basil cycle, bake, let cool, and serve.

Nutrition/ slice:

- calories 102, fat 3, fiber 4, carbs 13, protein 4

101. Jewish Bread

- Time spent preparing: two hours and ten minutes
- One hour is needed for cooking.
- One bread dish is served.

Ingredients:

- 1 egg yolk, whisked
- 1 egg white, whisked
- 2 teaspoons salt
- 250 g of hot water
- Half a cup of honey
- Two tsp olive oil
- Four cups of white flour
- Two tsp bread machine yeast

Directions:

1. In your bread machine, combine the flour, yeast, and remaining ingredients. Start the machine, add the light crust, and set it to the Basil cycle.
2. Stop the machine after the last rise is finished, put the dough on a floured surface, and gently knead it.
3. Divide the dough in half, then wrap each half into a long rope, braiding the ends together and tucking them in.
4. After inserting the bread, continue the cycle in the bread machine.
5. Serve once cooled.

Nutrition/ loaf:

- calories 200, fat 7, fiber 3, carbs 20, protein 7

102. Italian Bread

- Time spent preparing: ten minutes
- One hour is needed for cooking.
- One loaf is served.

Ingredients:

- 4 garlic cloves, minced
- 3 tablespoons soft butter
- 1 bulb roasted garlic
- 1 cup milk
- 100 g cheddar, grated
- three cups of white bread flour
- Two tablespoons sugar, one teaspoon salt, and one teaspoon garlic powder

- 1 teaspoon dry active yeast

Directions:

1. Squeeze the roasted garlic, then crush the cloves in a basin.
2. Combine all the remaining ingredients in your bread machine, select the Basic White cycle and Medium Crust, and begin the program.
3. Add the roasted garlic as well, after the last kneading cycle begins.
4. Before serving, prepare and chill the bread.

Nutrition/ slice:

- calories 140
- fat 4
- fiber 3
- carbs 16
- protein 4

103.   Veggie Bread

- Time spent preparing: ten minutes
- Two hours are needed for cooking.
- One loaf is served.

Ingredients:

- ¼ cup spring onions, chopped
- 100 g water
- ¼ cup green bell pepper, chopped
- 35 g chives, chopped
- two cups of white flour
- One spoonful of butter
- One teaspoon of seasoning, Creole
- One teaspoon each of salt, and active dry yeast
- 3 g sugar

Directions:

1. In the bread machine, mix all the ingredients, select the white bread cycle and medium crust and start the machine.
2. Cool the bread down and serve.

Nutrition/ slice:

- calories 47, fat 3, fiber 3, carbs 7, protein 1

104.   Oatmeal Bread

- Time spent preparing: ten minutes
- 2 hours and 30 minutes of cooking
- One loaf is served.

Ingredients:

- two tsp salt
- two tablespoons softened butter
- 250 g of hot water
- three tbsp honey
- One spoonful of molasses
- 100 g old-fashioned oats
- 1 egg, whisked
- 2 teaspoons dry yeast

Directions:

1. Blend together all the ingredients in your bread maker.
2. Press the start button after putting the machine in the White bread cycle with Medium crust.
3. Once baked, allow it cool before serving.

Nutrition/ slice:

- calories 162, fat 7, fiber 4, carbs 17, protein 5

105.   Romano Cheese Bread

- Time spent preparing: ten minutes
- Two hours are needed for cooking.
- One loaf is served.

Ingredients:

- 1 cup water
- 100 g Romano cheese, shredded
- 3 cups white flour
- 1 tablespoon oregano, chopped
- 35 g sugar
- One tsp salt and one tsp black pepper
- 2 teaspoons active yeast
- Two tbsp olive oil

Directions:

1. In your bread machine, combine the flour with the other ingredients. Select the White bread cycle and the light crust setting. Press the start button.

2. Slice, cool, and serve the bread.

Nutrition/slice:

- calories 70, fat 3, fiber 3, carbs 7, protein 2

106. Cheddar, Olives and Tomato Bread

- Time spent preparing: ten minutes
- One hour is needed for cooking.
- One loaf is served.

Ingredients:

- 100 g cheddar cheese, grated
- 3 tablespoons black olives, pitted and sliced
- 100 g sun-dried tomatoes, chopped
- 3 tablespoons soft butter
- 1 cup milk
- three cups of white bread flour
- One tsp salt
- One teaspoon dry active yeast and two tablespoons sugar

Directions:

1. In your bread machine, mix the cheese with the olives and the other ingredients, set the machine on Basic White cycle and Medium Crust and start the program.
2. Make the bread and cool down before serving.

Nutrition/ slice:

- calories 130, fat 3.2, fiber 3, carbs 11.6, protein 4

107. Parmesan and Cucumber Bread

- Time spent preparing: ten minutes
- Two hours are needed for cooking.
- One loaf is served.

Ingredients:

- Two tsp olive oil
- Grated 100 g parmesan
- 1 cup cucumber, minced
- 1 and 100 gs water, warm
- One tsp salt
- Two tsp of dry active yeast

- Four cups of white flour

Directions:

1. Combine all the ingredients in your bread machine, choose the medium crust and basil cycle, bake, let cool, and serve.

Nutrition/ slice:

- calories 132, fat 4.5, fiber 3.2, carbs 13, protein 4

108. Spring Onions and Zucchini Bread

- Time spent preparing: ten minutes
- Two hours are needed for cooking.
- One loaf is served.

Ingredients:

- ¼ cup spring onions, chopped
- 100 g water
- ¼ cup spring onions, chopped
- three cups of bread flour
- One tablespoon of olive oil
- One tsp salt and one tsp active dry yeast

Directions:

1. Combine all the ingredients in the bread maker, choose the medium crust and white bread cycle, and turn it on.
2. After the bread has cooled, serve.

Nutrition/ slice:

- calories 87, fat 6.5, fiber 3, carbs 7, protein 3.4

109. Milk and Basil Bread

- Time spent preparing: ten minutes
- Two hours are needed for cooking.
- One loaf is served.

Ingredients:

- 1 cup almond milk
- One spoonful of sugar
- One tablespoon of finely chopped basil
- three tablespoons softened butter
- three cups of bread flour

- One tsp salt
- two tsp dry machine yeast

Directions:

1. In the bread machine, mix the milk with the sugar and the other ingredients, chose the white bread setting and medium crust and start the machine.
2. Cool down and serve.

Nutrition/ slice:

- calories 100, fat 3, fiber 4, carbs 7, protein 3

110. Mint Bread

- Time spent preparing: ten minutes
- Two hours are needed for cooking.
- One loaf is served.

Ingredients:

- 250 g of hot water
- One tablespoon minced mint and three tablespoons honey
- Three teaspoons coconut oil, three and a half cups melted white flour
- One tsp salt
- two tsp dry machine yeast

Directions:

1. In a bread machine fitted with a warm water setting, combine the remaining ingredients with the mint. To make white bread, use the medium crust option. To begin, click the button.
2. After cooling, serve.

Nutrition/ slice:

- calories 70, fat 3, fiber 2.3, carbs 7, protein 2

111. Sourdough Brownies

- Twenty minutes for preparation
- 40 minutes for cooking
- One hour in total
- Serves: 8–10

Ingredients

- 100 g (120 mL) active sourdough starter
- 100 g (120 mL) unsalted butter

- 12 oz (355 ml) or 350 g of chocolate chips
- 100 g (120 mL) cocoa powder
- 2 tsp (10 ml) vanilla extract
- 2 large eggs plus one egg yolk
- 1 cup (235mL) white sugar
- 100 g (120mL) brown sugar, packed
- 1 cup (235mL) all-purpose flour
- 1 tsp (5 ml) salt

Directions:

1. Preheat the oven to 175 degrees Celsius (350 degrees Fahrenheit).
2. Heat the chocolate chips and butter in a microwave-safe dish for 30 seconds at a time, stirring every 30 seconds. Mix in the brown sugar and chocolate powder.
3. After that, mix in the vanilla extract. Use an electric mixer to whip the sugar and eggs in a large, separate bowl until they are pale and foamy, about 5 to 10 minutes.
4. Mix well after adding your starting and melting chocolate mixture. Stir in salt and flour gradually until well mixed.
5. You may now opt to incorporate chocolate bits, almonds, or additional ingredients if you so desire.
6. Transfer the mixture onto a parchment paper-lined baking dish, use a spatula to level the top if needed, and bake for 35 to 40 minutes.
7. Once cut into squares, serve anyway you like.

112.   Cinnamon Streusel Sourdough Coffee Cake

- Twenty minutes for preparation
- 45 minutes for cooking
- One hour and five minutes total
- Serves: 8–10

Ingredients

- 1 cup (235mL) active sourdough starter
- Two cups of all-purpose flour (475 mL)
- 235 mL (1 cup) of white sugar
- 2 large eggs
- 1 tsp (5 ml) essence de vanilla
- ¼ cup (60mL) Greek yogurt or sour cream
- 100 g (120mL) softened unsalted butter
- One tsp (5 ml) of raising agent

- ½ tsp (3 ml) baking soda
- ½ tsp (3 ml) salt
- ¼ cup (60 mL) milk
- 100 g (120 ml) icing sugar

Directions:

1. Preheat the oven to 175 degrees Celsius (350 degrees Fahrenheit).
2. Combine the sugar and butter and beat with an electric mixer until the mixture is completely combined and starts to lighten in color. The eggs, starter, and vanilla should be beaten in one more time.
3. In a different bowl, mix the dry ingredients.
4. After you add half of the dry ingredients to the wet mixture, stir until barely mixed.
5. Toss in the sour cream or yogurt.
6. As a last step, gradually incorporate the remaining dry ingredients, spoonful by spoon.
7. Here you will whip up the cinnamon topping.

   - ⅓ cup (80mL) melted unsalted butter
   - 3 tbsp (45 ml) all-purpose flour
   - 3 tsp (15 ml) ground cinnamon
   - ¾ cup (175mL) brown sugar, packed)

8. Blend until well blended.
9. Pour about half of the batter onto a baking pan that has been oiled.
10. Distribute half of the cinnamon topping onto the surface.
11. With the remaining batter and topping, repeat these layers.
12. It is preferable to add dollops of batter before attempting to distribute it uniformly because the batter is thick.
13. Bake for 40–45 minutes, or until a toothpick inserted into the center comes out clean.
14. Mix 100 g icing sugar with either milk or water to create a drizzle glaze.

113. Sourdough Pancakes with Orange Marmalade

- Twenty minutes for preparation
- Time of Rise: Twelve Hours
- 30 minutes for cooking
- Twelve hours and fifty minutes total
- Serves: 6

Ingredients

- 1 cup (235mL) active sourdough starter
- Two cups of all-purpose flour (475 mL)
- 2 cups (475 mL) buttermilk
- 2 tbsp (30 ml) white sugar

Directions:

1. Stir until well blended, cover, and let sit overnight at room temperature. In the morning, mix your batter with two big eggs, one orange's zest, one tsp (5 ml) baking soda, ¾ tsp (4 ml) salt, and four tablespoons (¼ cup/60 mL) melted butter.
2. Mix the ingredients together and cook the pancakes on a skillet that has been lightly oiled. Flip the pancakes once you notice that the bubbles in the batter have burst. Waffles may also be made using this same batter.
3. Accompany with fresh orange slices and orange marmalade.

Note: you can use plant milk soured with 3 g vinegar per cup to substitute for butter milk.

114.   Boysenberry Stuffed Sourdough Beignets

- Prep Time: 1 hour
- Rising Time: 16-18 hours
- Cooking Time: 1 hour
- Total Time: 18-20 hours
- Serves: 6-8

Ingredients

- 1 cup (235 mL) active sourdough starter
- 3 cups (710 mL) all purpose flour
- ¼ cup (60 mL) granulated sugar
- 1 tsp (5 ml) salt
- 2 tbsp (30 ml) butter, melted
- ¾ cup (175mL) buttermilk

Directions:

1. Mix flour, sugar, butter, starter, buttermilk, and salt. Mix or knead for 5 to 10 minutes, or until well blended into a sticky ball.
2. Move to a bowl, cover with plastic wrap, and allow to ferment for four to six hours, or until doubled.
3. After pounding, refrigerate for the entire night.

4. Meanwhile, get your jam ready. You may use any fruit that you have on hand, however we're choosing boysenberries. Or experiment with other jam tastes!

- Approximately 6 pounds (2 ¾ kg) berries
- 4 100 gs (1065mL) white or raw sugar
- Juice of one lemon
- 1 tsp (5 ml) butter

5. Put all the ingredients in a pot, cover, and simmer for around thirty minutes.
6. Simmer for a another half-hour; it should thicken significantly.
7. When the desired thickness is reached, remove from fire and let cool.
8. Roll out the dough to a thickness of ¼ inch in the morning, and then cut it into squares that are about 3 by 3 inches each.
9. Heat two inches of oil in a large saucepan to a temperature of about 325°F (165°C).
10.   Make sure the oil you're using—like canola or safflower oil—can tolerate high heat.
11.   Fry each beignet for a few seconds on each side, or until golden brown, using a spatula or slotted spoon.
12.   After cooking, place the beignets on a cooling rack.
13.   Make a tiny incision in the middle of each beignet using a pastry bag fitted with a tip, then pipe in jam until it just starts to come out of the hole.
14.   Once you sprinkle powdered sugar over your beignets, they're ready to be consumed!

115.   Chai Spice Monkey Sourdough Bread

- Thirty minutes for preparation
- Getting Up: 16–18 hours
- Takes 30 to 35 minutes to cook.
- Total Time: 17-19 hours
- Serves: 6-8

Ingredients

- 100g active sourdough starter (⅓ cup/80 ml) (70-80% hydration)
- 550 mL or two-thirds cup all-purpose flour
- 3 tbsp (45 ml) white sugar
- 1 tsp (5 ml) salt
- 1 egg
- 2 tbsp (30 ml) softened butter
- 100 g (120 mL) milk
- ½ tsp (3 ml)vanilla extract

- 2-3 tbsp (30-45 ml) extra water as needed

Directions:

1. Mix everything but the water in a dish.
2. Add water gradually to bring the dough together after mixing.
3. in a bowl and let ferment for 4–6 hours in a warm place after kneading on a floured surface until smooth.
4. Mash, roll into a ball, and refrigerate overnight.
5. In the morning, reheat the dough to room temperature and set the oven to 350°F (175°C).
6. Roll the dough to ½ inch thickness on a floured board, then cut into small squares.
7. Squares needn't be the same size. Next, prepare your coating:

- 100 g (120 mL) brown sugar
- ⅓ cup (80 mL) white sugar
- 1 tsp (5 ml) ground cinnamon
- ⅓ tsp (1 ml) ground ginger
- ½ tsp (3 ml) gound cardamom
- ¼ tsp (2 ml) ground cloves
- Small pinch black pepper
- 1 stick butter (100 g-120 mL), melted

8. Combine all coating ingredients. In a bundt pan or bread tin, arrange your dough pieces, then pour your coating mixture evenly on top. Bake for 30-35 minutes.

116.   Orange Sourdough Bread

- Prep Time: 1 hour
- Resting Time: 14 hours
- Rising Time: 1-2 hours
- Cooking Time: 45 minutes
- Total Time: 17-18 hours
- Serves: 8

Ingredients

- ¾ cup (175 ml) sourdough starter
- 15 ml orange zest
- 1 ¼ cup (295 ml) water
- 2 cups (475 ml) all-purpose flour
- 1 ¼ teaspoons (6 ml) sea salt

Directions:

1. In a large basin, combine the sourdough starter, water, and zest of oranges. The all-purpose flour should then be added and mixed until a shaggy dough forms.
2. After covering the sourdough with a fresh, moist kitchen towel, leave it alone for half an hour.
3. Dredge the sough dough in the sea salt, then lift the upper part of the dough, stretch it upward, and bring it to the middle of the bowl.
4. After rotating the bowl 90 degrees, pull the sourdough bread dough up and over the bowl's center.
5. After 30 minutes of resting the sourdough, repeat steps 3 and 4 and give the dough another 30 minutes to rest.
6. After one last time, repeat steps 3 and 4 and let the sourdough rest for half an hour.
7. Cover the orange sourdough with a clean, wet kitchen towel and let overnight at room temperature.
8. Shape the sourdough into a round loaf on a floured surface.
9. Cover the dough with a floured kitchen towel in a bowl. Let the dough rise for 1-2 hours.
10. Place a covered Dutch oven pot in the oven at 475°F (245°C).
11. Carefully transfer the sourdough bread onto a parchment paper center using a sharp knife or razor blade.
12. Carefully slide the parchment paper into the Dutch oven after removing the oven rack and cover.
13. Bake the Dutch oven for 30 minutes after covering. Remove the Dutch oven lid and bake for 10–15 minutes.
14. To cool completely, lay orange sourdough bread on a wire rack.

117.   Cranberry Walnut Sourdough Bread

- Get ready in 20 minutes
- Resting Time: 7½-8½ hours
- Rising Time: 1-2hrs
- Cook: 35–45 minutes
- Duration: 1 day
- Servings: 16

Ingredients

- ½ (120 ml) cup sourdough starter
- 1-1/2 cups (295 ml) room-temperature water
- 700 ml/3 cups Bread flour: ¼ cup (60 ml) whole wheat flour

- 1 ¼ teaspoons (6 ml) fine sea salt
- ¾ cup (175 ml) walnuts, shelled, toasted, chopped
- 100 g (120 ml) cranberries, sweetened

Directions:

1. In a large basin, mix the starter and water with the bread flour and whole wheat flour until no dry flour patches remain and loose dough forms.
2. The sourdough bread dough should be covered with sea salt, covered with a fresh, wet kitchen towel, and allowed to rest for an hour.
3. Water should be applied to your fingertips after removing the towel from the sourdough dough.
4. Scoop up the upper part of the dough, extend it upward, and bring it over the bowl's center.
5. After rotating the bowl 90 degrees, pull the sourdough bread dough up and over the bowl's center.
6. After 30 minutes of resting the sourdough, repeat steps 4 and 5 and give the dough another 30 minutes to rest.
7. After one last time, repeat steps 4 and 5 and let the sourdough rest for half an hour.
8. Transfer the sourdough to a surface dusted with flour, then carefully flatten it into a rectangle about 12 by 14 inches.
9. After pressing the cranberries and walnuts into the dough, sprinkle them over the sourdough, leaving a ½-inch border.
10. Pull one side over ½ and the other over the dough to form a log shape. Once the dough has been shaped into a circle, place it back in the basin, cover it with a clean, moist towel, and allow it to rest for five to six hours, or until it has doubled.
11. Once the dough has been floured, let it sit for 12 minutes. Sourdough should be divided in half, rolled into a log, and the ends sealed with a pinch.
12. Spoon dough into two loaf pans, cover with plastic wrap sprayed with nonstick cooking spray, and leave to rise for one to two hours.
13. Put a roasting pan on the lowest rack in an oven set at 425°F (220°C) and fill it with water.
14. Bake the cranberry-walnut sourdough bread for 15 to 20 minutes.
15. Lower the oven's temperature to 350°F and bake until golden brown, 20 to 25 minutes.
16. Give the loaves two to three minutes to cool in the pan.
17. Before slicing, allow the cranberry walnut sourdough bread to cool for one to two hours on a wire rack.

118. Goji Berry Pine Nut Sourdough Bread

- Get ready in 20 minutes
- Rest Time: 6-8 hours
- 30 minutes to rise
- Cook: 45 minutes
- Approximately 8-10 hours
- Serves 4

Ingredients:

- 1 cup wholegrain spelt flour
- 3 Tbsp sunflower seeds ground
- 35 g ground flax seeds
- A teaspoon (5 ml) salt
- 30 ml/2 tablespoon granular sugar
- 235 ml cup sourdough starter
- ¾ cup (175 ml) dried Goji berries
- 100 g (120 ml) toasted pine nuts, chopped
- 100 g (120 ml) of lukewarm water + 35 g (30 ml) water

Directions:

1. After sifting the spelt flour into a large basin, mix in the crushed sunflower seeds, flax seeds, salt, granulated sugar (one tablespoon), pine nuts, and Goji berries. Don't forget to save some pine nuts for the loaf's top.
2. Combine the sourdough starter, two tablespoons of water, and the last tablespoon of sugar in a another basin.
3. When a soft, smooth dough develops, add the starter to the sourdough along with the remaining 100 g of water and stir.
4. The sourdough should be rolled into a ball, put in a bowl that has been oiled, cover with clingfilm, and leave to rest for at least 6 to 8 hours or overnight.
5. Scoop up the upper part of the dough, extend it upward, and bring it over the bowl's center.
6. After rotating the bowl 90 degrees, pull the sourdough bread dough up and over the bowl's center.
7. Give the sourdough 30 minutes to rest.
8. Repeat steps 5 and 6, shape into a circular loaf, top with pine nuts, and let rise for 30 minutes.
9. Place a covered Dutch oven pot in the oven at 475°F (245°C).
10. Before scoring the top of the loaf, carefully place it in the middle of a sheet of parchment paper.
11. After taking the Dutch oven's cover and rack out, carefully slide the parchment paper inside.

12. After covering the Dutch oven, bake it for 30 minutes. Take the lid off the Dutch oven and bake it for ten to fifteen minutes.

13. The sourdough bread with goji berries, pine nuts, and a wire rack will cool entirely.

119. Chocolate Sourdough Bread

- Get ready in 20 minutes
- Rest: 3 hrs
- Rising Time: 9-13h
- Cook: 1 hour
- Total: 13-17 hrs
- Serves: 8

Ingredients

- ⅓ cup (80 ml) sourdough starter
- 1 100 gs (355 ml)water
- 3 cups (710 ml) white bread flour
- 100 g (120 ml) cocoa powder
- ¼ cup (60 ml) sugar
- 1 ¾ teaspoon (9 ml) sea salt
- 1 ½ tablespoons (22 ml) water

Ingredients

1. Combine sourdough starter and 1100 gs water in a large bowl. Shaggy dough is made by mixing bread flour, cocoa powder, and sugar.
2. Work the sourdough for 5 minutes on a floured surface.
3. Return the chocolate sourdough to the bowl, cover with a damp cloth, and rest for 30 minutes.
4. Combine sea salt and remaining water in the bowl.
5. Stretch the top dough and bring it over the basin.
6. Stretch the sourdough bread dough upward and over the basin centre after turning the bowl 90 degrees.
7. Place the chocolate sourdough under a clean wet kitchen towel for 30 minutes, then repeat steps 5 and 6 and let it rest for 30 minutes.
8. Finally, repeat steps 5 and 6 and let the sourdough rest for an hour.
9. Once the sourdough has rested for half an hour on a slightly floured surface, shape it into an oval or round loaf and transfer it to a sizable dish covered with a fresh kitchen towel. Place the sourdough loaf in the refrigerator and cover it with plastic wrap sprayed with nonstick cooking spray for 8 to 12 hours.

10.   Remove the chocolate sourdough from the refrigerator and let it sit for one hour.
11.   At 425°F (220°C), place a covered Dutch oven pot in the oven.
12.   Using a sharp knife or razor blade, carefully turn the sourdough bread onto parchment paper and slice the top.
13.   After removing the lid and oven rack, carefully place the edges of the parchment paper inside the Dutch oven.
14.   Bake the Dutch oven for 35 minutes with a cover on. Bake the chocolate sourdough bread for a further twenty-five minutes without the top.
15.   Chocolate sourdough bread must cool completely on a wire rack before slicing.

120.   Cherry Sourdough Bread

- Spend 30 minutes preparing
- Downtime: 6½-7½ hours
- Rising Time: 1-2hrs
- Cook: 45 minutes
- Total: 9-11 hrs
- Servings: 8

Ingredients

- 1/2 cup (120 ml) sourdough starter
- 1 ¼ cups (295 ml) water
- ¼ cup (60 ml) whole wheat flour and 3 cups (710 ml) bread flour
- 1 ¼ teaspoons (6 ml) fine sea salt
- ¾ cup (175 ml) dried cherries, soaked in water for 20 minutes, and drained

Directions:

1. Mix starter, water, whole wheat flour, and bread flour in a large bowl until a loose dough forms without dry patches.
2. Let the dough rest for an hour with a moist kitchen towel and sea salt.
3. After removing the dough cloth, wet your fingertips.
4. Stretch the top dough over the bowl.
5. Spread dough in the center after turning the bowl 90 degrees.
6. Restart steps 4 and 5 after 30 minutes and let the dough rest.
7. After finishing, repeat steps 4 and 5 and let the sourdough rest for 30 minutes.
8. Sprinkle flour on a surface and gently push sourdough into a 12-by-14-inch rectangle.
9. Apply dried cherries to sourdough, leaving a ½-inch border, and press into dough.

10. Form a log shape by pulling one side over ½ and the other over the dough. Roll the dough into a circle, return it to the bowl, cover it with a moist cloth, and let it rest for five to six hours until it doubles in size.

11. After resting for 12 minutes on a floured board, form the dough into a round loaf.

12. Sprinkle flour on dough in a dish lined with clean kitchen towels. Let dough rise 1–2 hours.

13. Preheat a covered Dutch oven pot to 475°F (245°C).

14. Turn the sourdough bread gently onto parchment paper and slice the top with a sharp knife or razor blade.

15. Grab the parchment paper edges and carefully place them in the Dutch oven after removing the rack and lid.

16. Bake the Dutch oven covered for 30 minutes. Continue baking for 10–15 minutes without the Dutch oven cover.

17. Cool cherry sourdough bread on a wire rack.

Conclusion

As we end "Sourdough Recipes Cookbook: A Step-by-Step Mastery Guide to No-Fail Baking and Crafting Healthful Breads, Sweets, and More with 120+ Recipes for All Skill Levels," we can reflect on our culinary journey Sourdough history, science, methodology, and 120 recipes are covered in this book. Each recipe, from simple loaves to complex desserts, was designed to improve your skills and confidence, making sourdough baking pleasurable for everyone.

This ebook offered step-by-step instructions and fail-safe healthy and delectable baking recipes. Well-tested recipes, clear instructions, and troubleshooting tips kept you on track. The book says sourdough's natural fermentation improves taste, digestibility, and nutrients. The manual makes sourdough baking fun and easy by fitting varied diets.

This book promotes sourdough baking empowerment. Understanding a timeless craft requires patience, inventiveness, and change. Sourdough baking calms us, is fun, and builds community by sharing our creations. As you continue your sourdough journey, may your kitchen smell like fresh bread and each loaf bring you delight.

BONUSES

What high-value exclusive bonuses I include in this book:

- **Bonus 1** – Video Tutorial No Knead Sourdough.
- **Bonus 2** - Video Tutorial Feeding Sourdough Starter - What to do with your new sourdough starter.
- **Bonus 3** - Video Tutorial for the ingredients for Sourdough Bread.
- **Bonus 4** – Video Tutorial Recipe for Sourdough Bread - How to weigh and mix it.
- **Bonus 5** – Video Tutorial How to Knead Sourdough Bread dough
- **Bonus 6** – Video Tutorial How to Shape Sourdough Bread
- **Bonus 7** – Video Tutorial How to Bake Sourdough Bread
- **Bonus 8** – Video Tutorial American Sourdough Bagels
- **Bonus 9** – Video Tutorial How to Make the Worlds Tastiest Sourdough bread

SCAN THE QR CODE BELOW
TO DOWNLOAD BONUS FOR FREE!

Made in the USA
Monee, IL
14 December 2024

73849323R00063